ARABIC
VOCABULARY

FOR ENGLISH SPEAKERS

ENGLISH-ARABIC

The most useful words
To expand your lexicon and sharpen
your language skills

3000 words

Arabic vocabulary for English speakers - 3000 words

By Andrey Taranov

T&P Books vocabularies are intended for helping you learn, memorize and review foreign words. The dictionary is divided into themes, covering all major spheres of everyday activities, business, science, culture, etc.

The process of learning words using T&P Books' theme-based dictionaries gives you the following advantages:

- Correctly grouped source information predetermines success at subsequent stages of word memorization
- Availability of words derived from the same root allowing memorization of word units (rather than separate words)
- Small units of words facilitate the process of establishing associative links needed for consolidation of vocabulary
- Level of language knowledge can be estimated by the number of learned words

T&P Books Publishing
www.tpbooks.com

ISBN: 978-1-78716-693-6

This book is also available in E-book formats.
Please visit www.tpbooks.com or the major online bookstores.

ARABIC VOCABULARY
for English speakers

T&P Books vocabularies are intended to help you learn, memorize, and review foreign words. The vocabulary contains over 3000 commonly used words arranged thematically.

- Vocabulary contains the most commonly used words
- Recommended as an addition to any language course
- Meets the needs of beginners and advanced learners of foreign languages
- Convenient for daily use, revision sessions, and self-testing activities
- Allows you to assess your vocabulary

Special features of the vocabulary

- Words are organized according to their meaning, not alphabetically
- Words are presented in three columns to facilitate the reviewing and self-testing processes
- Words in groups are divided into small blocks to facilitate the learning process
- The vocabulary offers a convenient and simple transcription of each foreign word

The vocabulary has 101 topics including:

Basic Concepts, Numbers, Colors, Months, Seasons, Units of Measurement, Clothing & Accessories, Food & Nutrition, Restaurant, Family Members, Relatives, Character, Feelings, Emotions, Diseases, City, Town, Sightseeing, Shopping, Money, House, Home, Office, Working in the Office, Import & Export, Marketing, Job Search, Sports, Education, Computer, Internet, Tools, Nature, Countries, Nationalities and more ...

T&P BOOKS' THEME-BASED DICTIONARIES

The Correct System for Memorizing Foreign Words

Acquiring vocabulary is one of the most important elements of learning a foreign language, because words allow us to express our thoughts, ask questions, and provide answers. An inadequate vocabulary can impede communication with a foreigner and make it difficult to understand a book or movie well.

The pace of activity in all spheres of modern life, including the learning of modern languages, has increased. Today, we need to memorize large amounts of information (grammar rules, foreign words, etc.) within a short period. However, this does not need to be difficult. All you need to do is to choose the right training materials, learn a few special techniques, and develop your individual training system.

Having a system is critical to the process of language learning. Many people fail to succeed in this regard; they cannot master a foreign language because they fail to follow a system comprised of selecting materials, organizing lessons, arranging new words to be learned, and so on. The lack of a system causes confusion and eventually, lowers self-confidence.

T&P Books' theme-based dictionaries can be included in the list of elements needed for creating an effective system for learning foreign words. These dictionaries were specially developed for learning purposes and are meant to help students effectively memorize words and expand their vocabulary.

Generally speaking, the process of learning words consists of three main elements:

- Reception (creation or acquisition) of a training material, such as a word list
- Work aimed at memorizing new words
- Work aimed at reviewing the learned words, such as self-testing

All three elements are equally important since they determine the quality of work and the final result. All three processes require certain skills and a well-thought-out approach.

New words are often encountered quite randomly when learning a foreign language and it may be difficult to include them all in a unified list. As a result, these words remain written on scraps of paper, in book margins, textbooks, and so on. In order to systematize such words, we have to create and continually update a "book of new words." A paper notebook, a netbook, or a tablet PC can be used for these purposes.

This "book of new words" will be your personal, unique list of words. However, it will only contain the words that you came across during the learning process. For example, you might have written down the words "Sunday," "Tuesday," and "Friday." However, there are additional words for days of the week, for example, "Saturday," that are missing, and your list of words would be incomplete. Using a theme dictionary, in addition to the "book of new words," is a reasonable solution to this problem.

The theme-based dictionary may serve as the basis for expanding your vocabulary.

It will be your big "book of new words" containing the most frequently used words of a foreign language already included. There are quite a few theme-based dictionaries available, and you should ensure that you make the right choice in order to get the maximum benefit from your purchase.

Therefore, we suggest using theme-based dictionaries from T&P Books Publishing as an aid to learning foreign words. Our books are specially developed for effective use in the sphere of vocabulary systematization, expansion and review.

Theme-based dictionaries are not a magical solution to learning new words. However, they can serve as your main database to aid foreign-language acquisition. Apart from theme dictionaries, you can have copybooks for writing down new words, flash cards, glossaries for various texts, as well as other resources; however, a good theme dictionary will always remain your primary collection of words.

T&P Books' theme-based dictionaries are specialty books that contain the most frequently used words in a language.

The main characteristic of such dictionaries is the division of words into themes. For example, the *City* theme contains the words "street," "crossroads," "square," "fountain," and so on. The *Talking* theme might contain words like "to talk," "to ask," "question," and "answer".

All the words in a theme are divided into smaller units, each comprising 3–5 words. Such an arrangement improves the perception of words and makes the learning process less tiresome. Each unit contains a selection of words with similar meanings or identical roots. This allows you to learn words in small groups and establish other associative links that have a positive effect on memorization.

The words on each page are placed in three columns: a word in your native language, its translation, and its transcription. Such positioning allows for the use of techniques for effective memorization. After closing the translation column, you can flip through and review foreign words, and vice versa. "This is an easy and convenient method of review – one that we recommend you do often."

Our theme-based dictionaries contain transcriptions for all the foreign words. Unfortunately, none of the existing transcriptions are able to convey the exact nuances of foreign pronunciation. That is why we recommend using the transcriptions only as a supplementary learning aid. Correct pronunciation can only be acquired with the help of sound. Therefore our collection includes audio theme-based dictionaries.

The process of learning words using T&P Books' theme-based dictionaries gives you the following advantages:

- You have correctly grouped source information, which predetermines your success at subsequent stages of word memorization
- Availability of words derived from the same root (lazy, lazily, lazybones), allowing you to memorize word units instead of separate words
- Small units of words facilitate the process of establishing associative links needed for consolidation of vocabulary
- You can estimate the number of learned words and hence your level of language knowledge
- The dictionary allows for the creation of an effective and high-quality revision process
- You can revise certain themes several times, modifying the revision methods and techniques
- Audio versions of the dictionaries help you to work out the pronunciation of words and develop your skills of auditory word perception

The T&P Books' theme-based dictionaries are offered in several variants differing in the number of words: 1.500, 3.000, 5.000, 7.000, and 9.000 words. There are also dictionaries containing 15,000 words for some language combinations. Your choice of dictionary will depend on your knowledge level and goals.

We sincerely believe that our dictionaries will become your trusty assistant in learning foreign languages and will allow you to easily acquire the necessary vocabulary.

TABLE OF CONTENTS

FAUNA 94

FLORA 101

COUNTRIES OF THE WORLD 105

PRONUNCIATION GUIDE

T&P phonetic alphabet	Arabic example	English example
[a]	[ṭaffa] طَفَّى	shorter than in ask
[ā]	[iχtār] إختار	calf, palm
[e]	[hamburger] هامبورجر	elm, medal
[i]	[zifāf] زفاف	shorter than in feet
[ī]	[abrīl] أبريل	feet, meter
[u]	[kalkutta] كلكتا	book
[ū]	[ʒāmūs] جاموس	fuel, tuna
[b]	[bidāya] بداية	baby, book
[d]	[saʿāda] سعادة	day, doctor
[ḍ]	[waḍʿ] وضع	[d] pharyngeal
[ʒ]	[arʒantīn] الأرجنتين	forge, pleasure
[ð]	[tiðkār] تذكار	pharyngealized th
[z̧]	[zahar] ظهر	[z] pharyngeal
[f]	[χafīf] خفيف	face, food
[g]	[gūlf] جولف	game, gold
[h]	[ittiʒāh] إتّجاه	home, have
[ḥ]	[aḥabb] أحبّ	[h] pharyngeal
[y]	[ðahabiy] ذهبيّ	yes, New York
[k]	[kursiy] كرسيّ	clock, kiss
[l]	[lamaḥ] لمح	lace, people
[m]	[marṣad] مرصد	magic, milk
[n]	[ʒanūb] جنوب	sang, thing
[p]	[kaputʃīnu] كابتشينو	pencil, private
[q]	[waθiq] وثق	king, club
[r]	[rūḥ] روح	rice, radio
[s]	[suχriyya] سخريّة	city, boss
[ṣ]	[miʿsam] معصم	[s] pharyngeal
[ʃ]	[ʿaʃāʾ] عشاء	machine, shark
[t]	[tannūb] تنّوب	tourist, trip
[ṭ]	[χarīṭa] خريطة	[t] pharyngeal
[θ]	[mamūθ] ماموث	month, tooth
[v]	[vitnām] فيتنام	very, river
[w]	[waddaʿ] ودّع	vase, winter
[χ]	[baχīl] بخيل	as in Scots 'loch'
[ɣ]	[taɣadda] تغدّى	between [g] and [h]
[z]	[māʿiz] ماعز	zebra, please

T&P phonetic alphabet	Arabic example	English example
['] (ayn)	سبعة [sab'a]	voiced pharyngeal fricative
['] (hamza)	سأل [sa'al]	glottal stop

ABBREVIATIONS
used in the vocabulary

Arabic abbreviations

du	-	plural noun (double)
f	-	feminine noun
m	-	masculine noun
pl	-	plural

English abbreviations

ab.	-	about
adj	-	adjective
adv	-	adverb
anim.	-	animate
as adj	-	attributive noun used as adjective
e.g.	-	for example
etc.	-	et cetera
fam.	-	familiar
fem.	-	feminine
form.	-	formal
inanim.	-	inanimate
masc.	-	masculine
math	-	mathematics
mil.	-	military
n	-	noun
pl	-	plural
pron.	-	pronoun
sb	-	somebody
sing.	-	singular
sth	-	something
v aux	-	auxiliary verb
vi	-	intransitive verb
vi, vt	-	intransitive, transitive verb
vt	-	transitive verb

BASIC CONCEPTS

1. Pronouns

I, me	ana	أنا
you (masc.)	anta	أنت
you (fem.)	anti	أنت
he	huwa	هو
she	hiya	هي
we	naḥnu	نحن
you (to a group)	antum	أنتم
they	hum	هم

2. Greetings. Salutations

Hello! (form.)	as salāmu 'alaykum!	السلام عليكم!
Good morning!	ṣabāḥ al ҳayr!	صباح الخير!
Good afternoon!	nahārak sa'īd!	نهارك سعيد!
Good evening!	masā' al ҳayr!	مساء الخير!
to say hello	sallam	سلّم
Hi! (hello)	salām!	سلام!
greeting (n)	salām (m)	سلام
to greet (vt)	sallam 'ala	سلّم على
How are you?	kayfa ḥāluka?	كيف حالك؟
What's new?	ma aҳbārak?	ما أخبارك؟
Bye-Bye! Goodbye!	ma' as salāma!	مع السلامة!
See you soon!	ilal liqā'!	إلى اللقاء!
Farewell!	ma' as salāma!	مع السلامة!
to say goodbye	wadda'	ودّع
So long!	bay bay!	باي باي!
Thank you!	ʃukran!	شكرًا!
Thank you very much!	ʃukran ʒazīlan!	شكرًا جزيلًا!
You're welcome	'afwan	عفوا
Don't mention it!	la ʃukr 'ala wāʒib	لا شكر على واجب
It was nothing	al 'afw	العفو
Excuse me! (fam.)	'an iðnak!	عن أذنك!
Excuse me! (form.)	'afwan!	عفوًا!
to excuse (forgive)	'aðar	عذر
to apologize (vi)	i'taðar	إعتذر

My apologies	ana 'āsif	أنا آسف
I'm sorry!	la tu'āẖiðni!	لا تؤاخذني!
to forgive (vt)	'afa	عفا
please (adv)	min faḍlak	من فضلك

Don't forget!	la tansa!	لا تنس!
Certainly!	ṭab'an!	طبعًا!
Of course not!	abadan!	أبدًا!
Okay! (I agree)	ittafaqna!	إتّفقنا!
That's enough!	kifāya!	كفاية!

3. Questions

Who?	man?	من؟
What?	māða?	ماذا؟
Where? (at, in)	ayna?	أين؟
Where (to)?	ila ayna?	إلى أين؟
From where?	min ayna?	من أين؟
When?	mata?	متى؟
Why? (What for?)	li māða?	لماذا؟
Why? (~ are you crying?)	li māða?	لماذا؟

What for?	li māða?	لماذا؟
How? (in what way)	kayfa?	كيف؟
What? (What kind of ...?)	ay?	أي؟
Which?	ay?	أي؟

To whom?	li man?	لمن؟
About whom?	'amman?	عمّن؟
About what?	'amma?	عمّا؟
With whom?	ma' man?	مع من؟

| How many? How much? | kam? | كم؟ |
| Whose? | li man? | لمن؟ |

4. Prepositions

with (accompanied by)	ma'	مع
without	bi dūn	بدون
to (indicating direction)	ila	إلى
about (talking ~ ...)	'an	عن
before (in time)	qabl	قبل
in front of ...	amām	أمام

under (beneath, below)	taḥt	تحت
above (over)	fawq	فوق
on (atop)	'ala	على
from (off, out of)	min	من

of (made from)	min	من
in (e.g., ~ ten minutes)	ba'd	بعد
over (across the top of)	'abr	عبر

5. Function words. Adverbs. Part 1

Where? (at, in)	ayna?	أين؟
here (adv)	huna	هنا
there (adv)	hunāk	هناك
somewhere (to be)	fi makānin ma	في مكان ما
nowhere (not anywhere)	la fi ay makān	لا في أي مكان
by (near, beside)	bi ʒānib	بجانب
by the window	bi ʒānib aʃ ʃubbāk	بجانب الشبّاك
Where (to)?	ila ayna?	إلى أين؟
here (e.g., come ~!)	huna	هنا
there (e.g., to go ~)	hunāk	هناك
from here (adv)	min huna	من هنا
from there (adv)	min hunāk	من هناك
close (adv)	qarīban	قريبًا
far (adv)	ba'īdan	بعيدًا
near (e.g., ~ Paris)	'ind	عند
nearby (adv)	qarīban	قريبًا
not far (adv)	ɣayr ba'īd	غير بعيد
left (adj)	al yasār	اليسار
on the left	'alaʃ ʃimāl	على الشمال
to the left	ilaʃ ʃimāl	إلى الشمال
right (adj)	al yamīn	اليمين
on the right	'alal yamīn	على اليمين
to the right	llal yamīn	إلى اليمين
in front (adv)	min al amām	من الأمام
front (as adj)	amāmiy	أمامي
ahead (the kids ran ~)	ilal amām	إلى الأمام
behind (adv)	warā'	وراء
from behind	min al warā'	من الوراء
back (towards the rear)	ilal warā'	إلى الوراء
middle	wasaṭ (m)	وسط
in the middle	fil wasat	في الوسط
at the side	bi ʒānib	بجانب
everywhere (adv)	fi kull makān	في كل مكان

around (in all directions)	ḥawl	حول
from inside	min ad dāχil	من الداخل
somewhere (to go)	ila ayy makān	إلى أيّ مكان
straight (directly)	bi aqṣar ṭarīq	بأقصر طريق
back (e.g., come ~)	ʼīyāban	إيابًا
from anywhere	min ayy makān	من أي مكان
from somewhere	min makānin ma	من مكان ما
firstly (adv)	awwalan	أوَّلًا
secondly (adv)	θāniyan	ثانيًا
thirdly (adv)	θāliθan	ثالثًا
suddenly (adv)	faʒʼa	فجأة
at first (in the beginning)	fil bidāya	في البداية
for the first time	li ʼawwal marra	لأوَّل مرَّة
long before ...	qabl ... bi mudda ṭawīla	قبل...بمدَّة طويلة
anew (over again)	min ʒadīd	من جديد
for good (adv)	ilal abad	إلى الأبد
never (adv)	abadan	أبدًا
again (adv)	min ʒadīd	من جديد
now (adv)	al ʼān	الآن
often (adv)	kaθīran	كثيرًا
then (adv)	fi ðalika al waqt	في ذلك الوقت
urgently (quickly)	ʼāʒilan	عاجلًا
usually (adv)	kal ʻāda	كالعادة
by the way, ...	ʻala fikra ...	على فكرة...
possible (that is ~)	min al mumkin	من الممكن
probably (adv)	laʻalla	لعلّ
maybe (adv)	min al mumkin	من الممكن
besides ...	bil iḍāfa ila ðalik ...	بالإضافة إلى...
that's why ...	li ðalik	لذلك
in spite of ...	bir raɣm min ...	بالرغم من...
thanks to ...	bi faḍl ...	بفضل...
what (pron.)	allaði	الذي
that (conj.)	anna	أنّ
something	ʃayʼ (m)	شيء
anything (something)	ʃayʼ (m)	شيء
nothing	la ʃayʼ	لا شيء
who (pron.)	allaði	الذي
someone	aḥad	أحد
somebody	aḥad	أحد
nobody	la aḥad	لا أحد
nowhere (a voyage to ~)	la ila ay makān	لا إلى أي مكان
nobody's	la yaχuṣṣ aḥad	لا يخص أحدًا
somebody's	li aḥad	لأحد
so (I'm ~ glad)	hakaða	هكذا

| also (as well) | kaðalika | كذلك |
| too (as well) | ayḍan | أيضًا |

6. Function words. Adverbs. Part 2

Why?	li māða?	لماذا؟
for some reason	li sababin ma	لسبب ما
because ...	li'anna ...	لأنّ...
for some purpose	li amr mā	لأمر ما

and	wa	و
or	aw	أو
but	lakin	لكن
for (e.g., ~ me)	li	لـ

too (~ many people)	kaθīran ӡiddan	كثير جدًا
only (exclusively)	faqaṭ	فقط
exactly (adv)	biḍ ḍabṭ	بالضبط
about (more or less)	naḥw	نحو

approximately (adv)	taqrīban	تقريبًا
approximate (adj)	taqrībiy	تقريبيّ
almost (adv)	taqrīban	تقريبًا
the rest	al bāqi (m)	الباقي

each (adj)	kull	كلّ
any (no matter which)	ayy	أيّ
many, much (a lot of)	kaθīr	كثير
many people	kaθīr min an nās	كثير من الناس
all (everyone)	kull an nās	كل الناس

in return for ...	muqābil ...	مقابل...
in exchange (adv)	muqābil	مقابل
by hand (made)	bil yad	باليد
hardly (negative opinion)	hayhāt	هيهات

probably (adv)	la'alla	لعلّ
on purpose (intentionally)	qaṣdan	قصدا
by accident (adv)	ṣudfa	صدفة

very (adv)	ӡiddan	جدًا
for example (adv)	maθalan	مثلا
between	bayn	بين
among	bayn	بين
so much (such a lot)	haðihi al kammiyya	هذه الكمية
especially (adv)	χāṣṣa	خاصّة

NUMBERS. MISCELLANEOUS

7. Cardinal numbers. Part 1

0 zero	ṣifr	صفر
1 one	wāḥid	واحد
1 one (fem.)	wāḥida	واحدة
2 two	iθnān	إثنان
3 three	θalāθa	ثلاثة
4 four	arba'a	أربعة
5 five	χamsa	خمسة
6 six	sitta	ستّة
7 seven	sab'a	سبعة
8 eight	θamāniya	ثمانية
9 nine	tis'a	تسعة
10 ten	'aʃara	عشرة
11 eleven	aḥad 'aʃar	أحد عشر
12 twelve	iθnā 'aʃar	إثنا عشر
13 thirteen	θalāθat 'aʃar	ثلاثة عشر
14 fourteen	arba'at 'aʃar	أربعة عشر
15 fifteen	χamsat 'aʃar	خمسة عشر
16 sixteen	sittat 'aʃar	ستّة عشر
17 seventeen	sab'at 'aʃar	سبعة عشر
18 eighteen	θamāniyat 'aʃar	ثمانية عشر
19 nineteen	tis'at 'aʃar	تسعة عشر
20 twenty	'iʃrūn	عشرون
21 twenty-one	wāḥid wa 'iʃrūn	واحد وعشرون
22 twenty-two	iθnān wa 'iʃrūn	إثنان وعشرون
23 twenty-three	θalāθa wa 'iʃrūn	ثلاثة وعشرون
30 thirty	θalāθīn	ثلاثون
31 thirty-one	wāḥid wa θalāθūn	واحد وثلاثون
32 thirty-two	iθnān wa θalāθūn	إثنان وثلاثون
33 thirty-three	θalāθa wa θalāθūn	ثلاثة وثلاثون
40 forty	arba'ūn	أربعون
41 forty-one	wāḥid wa arba'ūn	واحد وأربعون
42 forty-two	iθnān wa arba'ūn	إثنان وأربعون
43 forty-three	θalāθa wa arba'ūn	ثلاثة وأربعون
50 fifty	χamsūn	خمسون
51 fifty-one	wāḥid wa χamsūn	واحد وخمسون

| 52 fifty-two | iθnān wa χamsūn | إثنان وخمسون |
| 53 fifty-three | θalāθa wa χamsūn | ثلاثة وخمسون |

60 sixty	sittūn	ستّون
61 sixty-one	wāḥid wa sittūn	واحد وستّون
62 sixty-two	iθnān wa sittūn	إثنان وستّون
63 sixty-three	θalāθa wa sittūn	ثلاثة وستّون

70 seventy	sab'ūn	سبعون
71 seventy-one	wāḥid wa sab'ūn	واحد وسبعون
72 seventy-two	iθnān wa sab'ūn	إثنان وسبعون
73 seventy-three	θalāθa wa sab'ūn	ثلاثة وسبعون

80 eighty	θamānūn	ثمانون
81 eighty-one	wāḥid wa θamānūn	واحد وثمانون
82 eighty-two	iθnān wa θamānūn	إثنان وثمانون
83 eighty-three	θalāθa wa θamānūn	ثلاثة وثمانون

90 ninety	tis'ūn	تسعون
91 ninety-one	wāḥid wa tis'ūn	واحد وتسعون
92 ninety-two	iθnān wa tis'ūn	إثنان وتسعون
93 ninety-three	θalāθa wa tis'ūn	ثلاثة وتسعون

8. Cardinal numbers. Part 2

100 one hundred	mi'a	مائة
200 two hundred	mi'atān	مائتان
300 three hundred	θalāθumi'a	ثلاثمائة
400 four hundred	rub'umi'a	أربعمائة
500 five hundred	χamsumi'a	خمسمائة

600 six hundred	sittumi'a	ستّمائة
700 seven hundred	sab'umi'a	سبعمائة
800 eight hundred	θamānimi'a	ثمانمائة
900 nine hundred	tis'umi'a	تسعمائة

1000 one thousand	alf	ألف
2000 two thousand	alfān	ألفان
3000 three thousand	θalāθat 'ālāf	ثلاثة آلاف
10000 ten thousand	'aʃarat 'ālāf	عشرة آلاف
one hundred thousand	mi'at alf	مائة ألف
million	milyūn (m)	مليون
billion	milyār (m)	مليار

9. Ordinal numbers

| first (adj) | awwal | أوَّل |
| second (adj) | θāni | ثان |

third (adj)	θāliθ	ثالث
fourth (adj)	rābiʿ	رابع
fifth (adj)	χāmis	خامس
sixth (adj)	sādis	سادس
seventh (adj)	sābiʿ	سابع
eighth (adj)	θāmin	ثامن
ninth (adj)	tāsiʿ	تاسع
tenth (adj)	ʿāʃir	عاشر

COLOURS. UNITS OF MEASUREMENT

10. Colors

color	lawn (m)	لون
shade (tint)	daraʒat al lawn (m)	درجة اللون
hue	ṣabɣit lūn (f)	لون
rainbow	qaws quzaḥ (m)	قوس قزح
white (adj)	abyaḍ	أبيض
black (adj)	aswad	أسود
gray (adj)	ramādiy	رماديَ
green (adj)	axḍar	أخضر
yellow (adj)	aṣfar	أصفر
red (adj)	aḥmar	أحمر
blue (adj)	azraq	أزرق
light blue (adj)	azraq fātiḥ	أزرق فاتح
pink (adj)	wardiy	ورديَ
orange (adj)	burtuqāliy	برتقاليَ
violet (adj)	banafsaʒiy	بنفسجيَ
brown (adj)	bunniy	بنّيَ
golden (adj)	ðahabiy	ذهبيَ
silvery (adj)	fiḍḍiy	فضيَ
beige (adj)	bɛ:ʒ	بيج
cream (adj)	ʿāʒiy	عاجيَ
turquoise (adj)	fayrūziy	فيروزيَ
cherry red (adj)	karaziy	كرزيَ
lilac (adj)	laylakiy	ليلكيَ
crimson (adj)	qirmiziy	قرمزيَ
light (adj)	fātiḥ	فاتح
dark (adj)	ɣāmiq	غامق
bright, vivid (adj)	zāhi	زاه
colored (pencils)	mulawwan	ملوّن
color (e.g., ~ film)	mulawwan	ملوّن
black-and-white (adj)	abyaḍ wa aswad	أبيض وأسود
plain (one-colored)	waḥīd al lawn, sāda	وحيد اللون, سادة
multicolored (adj)	mutaʿaddid al alwān	متعدّد الألوان

11. Units of measurement

weight	wazn (m)	وزن
length	ṭūl (m)	طول
width	'arḍ (m)	عرض
height	irtifā' (m)	إرتفاع
depth	'umq (m)	عمق
volume	ḥaʒm (m)	حجم
area	misāḥa (f)	مساحة

gram	grām (m)	جرام
milligram	milliɣrām (m)	مليغرام
kilogram	kiluɣrām (m)	كيلوغرام
ton	ṭunn (m)	طنّ
pound	raṭl (m)	رطل
ounce	ūnṣa (f)	أونصة

meter	mitr (m)	متر
millimeter	millimitr (m)	مليمتر
centimeter	santimitr (m)	سنتيمتر
kilometer	kilumitr (m)	كيلومتر
mile	mīl (m)	ميل

inch	būṣa (f)	بوصة
foot	qadam (f)	قدم
yard	yārda (f)	ياردة

| square meter | mitr murabba' (m) | متر مربّع |
| hectare | hiktār (m) | هكتار |

liter	litr (m)	لتر
degree	daraʒa (f)	درجة
volt	vūlt (m)	فولت
ampere	ambīr (m)	أمبير
horsepower	ḥiṣān (m)	حصان

quantity	kammiyya (f)	كمّية
a little bit of ...	qalīl ...	قليل...
half	niṣf (m)	نصف

| dozen | iθnā 'aʃar (f) | إثنا عشر |
| piece (item) | waḥda (f) | وحدة |

| size | ḥaʒm (m) | حجم |
| scale (map ~) | miqyās (m) | مقياس |

minimal (adj)	al adna	الأدنى
the smallest (adj)	al aṣɣar	الأصغر
medium (adj)	mutawassiṭ	متوسّط
maximal (adj)	al aqṣa	الأقصى
the largest (adj)	al akbar	الأكبر

12. Containers

canning jar (glass ~)	barṭamān (m)	برطمان
can	tanaka (f)	تنكة
bucket	ӡardal (m)	جردل
barrel	barmīl (m)	برميل
wash basin (e.g., plastic ~)	ḥawḍ lil ɣasīl (m)	حوض للغسيل
tank (100L water ~)	xazzān (m)	خزّان
hip flask	zamzamiyya (f)	زمزميّة
jerrycan	ӡirikan (m)	جركن
tank (e.g., tank car)	xazzān (m)	خزّان
mug	māgg (m)	ماجّ
cup (of coffee, etc.)	finӡān (m)	فنجان
saucer	ṭabaq finӡān (m)	طبق فنجان
glass (tumbler)	kubbāya (f)	كبّاية
wine glass	ka's (f)	كأس
stock pot (soup pot)	kassirūlla (f)	كاسرولة
bottle (~ of wine)	zuӡāӡa (f)	زجاجة
neck (of the bottle, etc.)	'unq (m)	عنق
carafe (decanter)	dawraq zuӡāӡiy (m)	دورق زجاجيّ
pitcher	ibrīq (m)	إبريق
vessel (container)	inā' (m)	إناء
pot (crock, stoneware ~)	aṣīṣ (m)	أصيص
vase	vāza (f)	فازة
bottle (perfume ~)	zuӡāӡa (f)	زجاجة
vial, small bottle	zuӡāӡa (f)	زجاجة
tube (of toothpaste)	umbūba (f)	أنبوبة
sack (bag)	kīs (m)	كيس
bag (paper ~, plastic ~)	kīs (m)	كيس
pack (of cigarettes, etc.)	'ulba (f)	علبة
box (e.g., shoebox)	'ulba (f)	علبة
crate	ṣundū' (m)	صندوق
basket	salla (f)	سلّة

MAIN VERBS

13. The most important verbs. Part 1

to advise (vt)	naṣaḥ	نصح
to agree (say yes)	ittafaq	إتّفق
to answer (vi, vt)	aʒāb	أجاب
to apologize (vi)	iʿtaðar	إعتذر
to arrive (vi)	waṣal	وصل
to ask (~ oneself)	sa'al	سأل
to ask (~ sb to do sth)	ṭalab	طلب
to be (vi)	kān	كان
to be afraid	χāf	خاف
to be hungry	arād an ya'kul	أراد أن يأكل
to be interested in …	ihtamm	إهتمّ
to be needed	kān maṭlūb	كان مطلوبا
to be surprised	indahaʃ	إندهش
to be thirsty	arād an yaʃrab	أراد أن يشرب
to begin (vt)	bada'	بدأ
to belong to …	χaṣṣ	خصّ
to boast (vi)	tabāha	تباهى
to break (split into pieces)	kasar	كسر
to call (~ for help)	istaɣāθ	إستغاث
can (v aux)	istaṭāʿ	إستطاع
to catch (vt)	amsak	أمسك
to change (vt)	ɣayyar	غيّر
to choose (select)	iχtār	إختار
to come down (the stairs)	nazil	نزل
to compare (vt)	qāran	قارن
to complain (vi, vt)	ʃaka	شكا
to confuse (mix up)	iχtalaṭ	إختلط
to continue (vt)	istamarr	إستمرّ
to control (vt)	taḥakkam	تحكّم
to cook (dinner)	ḥaḍḍar	حضّر
to cost (vt)	kallaf	كلّف
to count (add up)	ʿadd	عدّ
to count on …	iʿtamad ʿala …	إعتمد على...
to create (vt)	χalaq	خلق
to cry (weep)	baka	بكى

14. The most important verbs. Part 2

to deceive (vi, vt)	χadaʿ	خدع
to decorate (tree, street)	zayyan	زيّن
to defend (a country, etc.)	dāfaʿ	دافع
to demand (request firmly)	ṭālib	طالب
to dig (vt)	ḥafar	حفر
to discuss (vt)	nāqaʃ	ناقش
to do (vt)	ʿamal	عمل
to doubt (have doubts)	ʃakk fi	شكّ في
to drop (let fall)	awqaʿ	أوقع
to enter (room, house, etc.)	daχal	دخل
to exist (vi)	kān mawʒūd	كان موجودًا
to expect (foresee)	tanabba'	تنبّأ
to explain (vt)	ʃaraḥ	شرح
to fall (vi)	saqaṭ	سقط
to find (vt)	waʒad	وجد
to finish (vt)	atamm	أتمّ
to fly (vi)	ṭār	طار
to follow ... (come after)	tabaʿ	تبع
to forget (vi, vt)	nasiy	نسي
to forgive (vt)	ʿafa	عفا
to give (vt)	aʿṭa	أعطى
to give a hint	aʿṭa talmīḥ	أعطى تلميحًا
to go (on foot)	maʃa	مشى
to go for a swim	sabaḥ	سبح
to go out (for dinner, etc.)	χaraʒ	خرج
to guess (the answer)	χamman	خمّن
to have (vt)	malak	ملك
to have breakfast	afṭar	أفطر
to have dinner	taʿaʃʃa	تعشّى
to have lunch	taɣadda	تغدّى
to hear (vt)	samiʿ	سمع
to help (vt)	sāʿad	ساعد
to hide (vt)	χaba'	خبأ
to hope (vi, vt)	tamanna	تمنّى
to hunt (vi, vt)	iṣṭād	إصطاد
to hurry (vi)	istaʿʒal	إستعجل

15. The most important verbs. Part 3

to inform (vt)	aχbar	أخبر
to insist (vi, vt)	aṣarr	أصرّ

to insult (vt)	ahān	أهان
to invite (vt)	da'a	دعا
to joke (vi)	mazaḥ	مزح
to keep (vt)	ḥafaẓ	حفظ
to keep silent	sakat	سكت
to kill (vt)	qatal	قتل
to know (sb)	'araf	عرف
to know (sth)	'araf	عرف
to laugh (vi)	ḍaḥik	ضحك
to liberate (city, etc.)	ḥarrar	حرّر
to like (I like …)	a'ʒab	أعجب
to look for … (search)	baḥaθ	بحث
to love (sb)	aḥabb	أحبّ
to make a mistake	aҳṭa'	أخطأ
to manage, to run	adār	أدار
to mean (signify)	'ana	عنى
to mention (talk about)	ðakar	ذكر
to miss (school, etc.)	ɣāb	غاب
to notice (see)	lāḥaẓ	لاحظ
to object (vi, vt)	i'taraḍ	إعترض
to observe (see)	rāqab	راقب
to open (vt)	fataḥ	فتح
to order (meal, etc.)	ṭalab	طلب
to order (mil.)	amar	أمر
to own (possess)	malak	ملك
to participate (vi)	iʃtarak	إشترك
to pay (vi, vt)	dafa'	دفع
to permit (vt)	raҳҳaṣ	رخّص
to plan (vt)	ҳaṭṭaṭ	خطّط
to play (children)	la'ib	لعب
to pray (vi, vt)	ṣalla	صلّى
to prefer (vt)	faḍḍal	فضّل
to promise (vt)	wa'ad	وعد
to pronounce (vt)	naṭaq	نطق
to propose (vt)	iqtaraḥ	إقترح
to punish (vt)	'āqab	عاقب

16. The most important verbs. Part 4

to read (vi, vt)	qara'	قرأ
to recommend (vt)	naṣaḥ	نصح
to refuse (vi, vt)	rafaḍ	رفض
to regret (be sorry)	nadim	ندم
to rent (sth from sb)	ista'ʒar	إستأجر

to repeat (say again)	karrar	كرّر
to reserve, to book	ḥaʒaz	حجز
to run (vi)	ʒara	جرى
to save (rescue)	anqaδ	أنقذ
to say (~ thank you)	qāl	قال
to scold (vt)	wabbaχ	وبّخ
to see (vt)	raʾa	رأى
to sell (vt)	bāʿ	باع
to send (vt)	arsal	أرسل
to shoot (vi)	aṭlaq an nār	أطلق النار
to shout (vi)	ṣaraχ	صرخ
to show (vt)	ʿaraḍ	عرض
to sign (document)	waqqaʿ	وقّع
to sit down (vi)	ʒalas	جلس
to smile (vi)	ibtasam	إبتسم
to speak (vi, vt)	takallam	تكلّم
to steal (money, etc.)	saraq	سرق
to stop (for pause, etc.)	waqaf	وقف
to stop (please ~ calling me)	tawaqqaf	توقّف
to study (vt)	daras	درس
to swim (vi)	sabaḥ	سبح
to take (vt)	aχaδ	أخذ
to think (vi, vt)	ẓann	ظنّ
to threaten (vt)	haddad	هدّد
to touch (with hands)	lamas	لمس
to translate (vt)	tarʒam	ترجم
to trust (vt)	waθiq	وثق
to try (attempt)	ḥāwal	حاول
to turn (e.g., ~ left)	inʿaṭaf	إنعطف
to underestimate (vt)	istaχaff	إستخفّ
to understand (vt)	fahim	فهم
to unite (vt)	waḥḥad	وحّد
to wait (vt)	inṭazar	إنتظر
to want (wish, desire)	arād	أراد
to warn (vt)	ḥaδδar	حذّر
to work (vi)	ʿamal	عمل
to write (vt)	katab	كتب
to write down	katab	كتب

TIME. CALENDAR

17. Weekdays

Monday	yawm al iθnayn (m)	يوم الإثنين
Tuesday	yawm aθ θulāθā' (m)	يوم الثلاثاء
Wednesday	yawm al arbi'ā' (m)	يوم الأربعاء
Thursday	yawm al χamīs (m)	يوم الخميس
Friday	yawm al ʒum'a (m)	يوم الجمعة
Saturday	yawm as sabt (m)	يوم السبت
Sunday	yawm al aḥad (m)	يوم الأحد
today (adv)	al yawm	اليوم
tomorrow (adv)	γadan	غداً
the day after tomorrow	ba'd γad	بعد غد
yesterday (adv)	ams	أمس
the day before yesterday	awwal ams	أوّل أمس
day	yawm (m)	يوم
working day	yawm 'amal (m)	يوم عمل
public holiday	yawm al 'uṭla ar rasmiyya (m)	يوم العطلة الرسمية
day off	yawm 'uṭla (m)	يوم عطلة
weekend	ayyām al 'uṭla (pl)	أيام العطلة
all day long	ṭūl al yawm	طول اليوم
the next day (adv)	fil yawm at tāli	في اليوم التالي
two days ago	min yawmayn	قبل يومين
the day before	fil yawm as sābiq	في اليوم السابق
daily (adj)	yawmiy	يومي
every day (adv)	yawmiyyan	يومياً
week	usbū' (m)	أسبوع
last week (adv)	fil isbū' al māḍi	في الأسبوع الماضي
next week (adv)	fil isbū' al qādim	في الأسبوع القادم
weekly (adj)	usbū'iy	أسبوعي
every week (adv)	usbū'iyyan	أسبوعياً
twice a week	marratayn fil usbū'	مرّتين في الأسبوع
every Tuesday	kull yawm aθ θulaθā'	كل يوم الثلاثاء

18. Hours. Day and night

morning	ṣabāḥ (m)	صباح
in the morning	fiṣ ṣabāḥ	في الصباح

noon, midday	ẓuhr (m)	ظهر
in the afternoon	ba'd aẓ ẓuhr	بعد الظهر
evening	masā' (m)	مساء
in the evening	fil masā'	في المساء
night	layl (m)	ليل
at night	bil layl	بالليل
midnight	muntaṣif al layl (m)	منتصف الليل
second	θāniya (f)	ثانية
minute	daqīqa (f)	دقيقة
hour	sā'a (f)	ساعة
half an hour	niṣf sā'a (m)	نصف ساعة
a quarter-hour	rub' sā'a (f)	ربع ساعة
fifteen minutes	xamsat 'aʃar daqīqa	خمس عشرة دقيقة
24 hours	yawm kāmil (m)	يوم كامل
sunrise	ʃurūq aʃ ʃams (m)	شروق الشمس
dawn	faʒr (m)	فجر
early morning	ṣabāḥ bākir (m)	صباح باكر
sunset	ɣurūb aʃ ʃams (m)	غروب الشمس
early in the morning	fis ṣabāḥ al bākir	في الصباح الباكر
this morning	al yawm fiṣ ṣabāḥ	اليوم في الصباح
tomorrow morning	ɣadan fiṣ ṣabāḥ	غدًا في الصباح
this afternoon	al yawm ba'd aẓ ẓuhr	اليوم بعد الظهر
in the afternoon	ba'd aẓ ẓuhr	بعد الظهر
tomorrow afternoon	ɣadan ba'd aẓ ẓuhr	غدًا بعد الظهر
tonight (this evening)	al yawm fil masā'	اليوم في المساء
tomorrow night	ɣadan fil masā'	غدًا في المساء
at 3 o'clock sharp	fis sā'a aθ θāliθa tamāman	في الساعة الثالثة تماما
about 4 o'clock	fis sā'a ar rābi'a taqrīban	في الساعة الرابعة تقريبا
by 12 o'clock	ḥattas sā'a aθ θāniya 'aʃara	حتى الساعة الثانية عشرة
in 20 minutes	ba'd 'iʃrīn daqīqa	بعد عشرين دقيقة
in an hour	ba'd sā'a	بعد ساعة
on time (adv)	fi maw'idih	في موعده
a quarter of ...	illa rub'	إلا ربع
within an hour	ṭiwāl sā'a	طوال الساعة
every 15 minutes	kull rub' sā'a	كل ربع ساعة
round the clock	layl nahār	ليل نهار

19. Months. Seasons

| January | yanāyir (m) | يناير |
| February | fibrāyir (m) | فبراير |

March	māris (m)	مارس
April	abrīl (m)	أبريل
May	māyu (m)	مايو
June	yūnyu (m)	يونيو
July	yūlyu (m)	يوليو
August	aɣusṭus (m)	أغسطس
September	sibtambar (m)	سبتمبر
October	uktūbir (m)	أكتوبر
November	nuvimbar (m)	نوفمبر
December	disimbar (m)	ديسمبر
spring	rabīʿ (m)	ربيع
in spring	fir rabīʿ	في الربيع
spring (as adj)	rabīʿiy	ربيعي
summer	ṣayf (m)	صيف
in summer	fiṣ ṣayf	في الصيف
summer (as adj)	ṣayfiy	صيفي
fall	χarīf (m)	خريف
in fall	fil χarīf	في الخريف
fall (as adj)	χarīfiy	خريفيَ
winter	ʃitāʾ (m)	شتاء
in winter	fiʃ ʃitāʾ	في الشتاء
winter (as adj)	ʃitawiy	شتويَ
month	ʃahr (m)	شهر
this month	fi haða aʃ ʃahr	في هذا الشهر
next month	fiʃ ʃahr al qādim	في الشهر القادم
last month	fiʃ ʃahr al māḍi	في الشهر الماضي
a month ago	qabl ʃahr	قبل شهر
in a month (a month later)	baʿd ʃahr	بعد شهر
in 2 months (2 months later)	baʿd ʃahrayn	بعد شهرين
the whole month	ṭūl aʃ ʃahr	طول الشهر
all month long	ʃahr kāmil	شهر كامل
monthly (~ magazine)	ʃahriy	شهريَ
monthly (adv)	kull ʃahr	كل شهر
every month	kull ʃahr	كل شهر
twice a month	marratayn fiʃ ʃahr	مرّتين في الشهر
year	sana (f)	سنة
this year	fi haðihi as sana	في هذه السنة
next year	fis sana al qādima	في السنة القادمة
last year	fis sana al māḍiya	في السنة الماضية
a year ago	qabla sana	قبل سنة
in a year	baʿd sana	بعد سنة

in two years	ba'd sanatayn	بعد سنتين
the whole year	ṭūl as sana	طول السنة
all year long	sana kāmila	سنة كاملة

every year	kull sana	كل سنة
annual (adj)	sanawiy	سنويّ
annually (adv)	kull sana	كل سنة
4 times a year	arba' marrāt fis sana	أربع مرّات في السنة

date (e.g., today's ~)	tarīχ (m)	تاريخ
date (e.g., ~ of birth)	tarīχ (m)	تاريخ
calendar	taqwīm (m)	تقويم

half a year	niṣf sana (m)	نصف سنة
six months	niṣf sana (m)	نصف سنة
season (summer, etc.)	faṣl (m)	فصل
century	qarn (m)	قرن

TRAVEL. HOTEL

20. Trip. Travel

tourism, travel	siyāḥa (f)	سياحة
tourist	sā'iḥ (m)	سائح
trip, voyage	riḥla (f)	رحلة

| adventure | muɣāmara (f) | مغامرة |
| trip, journey | riḥla (f) | رحلة |

vacation	'uṭla (f)	عطلة
to be on vacation	'indahu 'uṭla	عنده عطلة
rest	istirāḥa (f)	إستراحة

train	qiṭār (m)	قطار
by train	bil qiṭār	بالقطار
airplane	ṭā'ira (f)	طائرة
by airplane	biṭ ṭā'ira	بالطائرة

| by car | bis sayyāra | بالسيّارة |
| by ship | bis safina | بالسفينة |

luggage	aʃ ʃunaṭ (pl)	الشنط
suitcase	ḥaqībat safar (f)	حقيبة سفر
luggage cart	'arabat ʃunaṭ (f)	عربة شنط

| passport | ʒawāz as safar (m) | جواز السفر |
| visa | ta'ʃīra (f) | تأشيرة |

| ticket | taðkira (f) | تذكرة |
| air ticket | taðkirat ṭā'ira (f) | تذكرة طائرة |

| guidebook | dalīl (m) | دليل |
| map (tourist ~) | χarīṭa (f) | خريطة |

| area (rural ~) | mintaqa (f) | منطقة |
| place, site | makān (m) | مكان |

exotica (n)	ɣarāba (f)	غرابة
exotic (adj)	ɣarīb	غريب
amazing (adj)	mudhiʃ	مدهش

group	maʒmū'a (f)	مجموعة
excursion, sightseeing tour	ʒawla (f)	جولة
guide (person)	murʃid (m)	مرشد

21. Hotel

| hotel | funduq (m) | فندق |
| motel | mutīl (m) | موتيل |

three-star (~ hotel)	θalāθat nuʒūm	ثلاثة نجوم
five-star	χamsat nuʒūm	خمسة نجوم
to stay (in a hotel, etc.)	nazal	نزل

room	ɣurfa (f)	غرفة
single room	ɣurfa li ʃaχṣ wāhid (f)	غرفة لشخص واحد
double room	ɣurfa li ʃaχṣayn (f)	غرفة لشخصين
to book a room	haʒaz ɣurfa	حجز غرفة

| half board | waʒbitān fil yawm (du) | وجبتان في اليوم |
| full board | θalāθ waʒabāt fil yawm | ثلاث وجبات في اليوم |

with bath	bi hawd al istihmām	بحوض الإستحمام
with shower	bid duʃ	بالدوش
satellite television	tilivizyūn faḍā'iy (m)	تلفزيون فضائيّ
air-conditioner	takyīf (m)	تكييف
towel	fūṭa (f)	فوطة
key	miftāh (m)	مفتاح

administrator	mudīr (m)	مدير
chambermaid	'āmilat tanzīf ɣuraf (f)	عاملة تنظيف غرف
porter, bellboy	hammāl (m)	حمّال
doorman	bawwāb (m)	بوّاب

restaurant	maṭ'am (m)	مطعم
pub, bar	bār (m)	بار
breakfast	fuṭūr (m)	فطور
dinner	'aʃā' (m)	عشاء
buffet	bufīh (m)	بوفيه

| lobby | radha (f) | ردهة |
| elevator | miṣ'ad (m) | مصعد |

| DO NOT DISTURB | ar raʒā' 'adam al iz'āʒ | الرجاء عدم الإزعاج |
| NO SMOKING | mamnū' at tadχīn | ممنوع التدخين |

22. Sightseeing

monument	timθāl (m)	تمثال
fortress	qal'a (f), hiṣn (m)	قلعة، حصن
palace	qaṣr (m)	قصر
castle	qal'a (f)	قلعة
tower	burʒ (m)	برج
mausoleum	ḍarīh (m)	ضريح

architecture	handasa miʿmāriyya (f)	هندسة معمارية
medieval (adj)	min al qurūn al wusṭa	من القرون الوسطى
ancient (adj)	qadīm	قديم
national (adj)	waṭaniy	وطني
famous (monument, etc.)	maʃhūr	مشهور

tourist	sāʾiḥ (m)	سائح
guide (person)	murʃid (m)	مرشد
excursion, sightseeing tour	ʒawla (f)	جولة
to show (vt)	ʿaraḍ	عرض
to tell (vt)	ḥaddaθ	حدّث

to find (vt)	waʒad	وجد
to get lost (lose one's way)	ḍāʿ	ضاع
map (e.g., subway ~)	χarīṭa (f)	خريطة
map (e.g., city ~)	χarīṭa (f)	خريطة

souvenir, gift	tiðkār (m)	تذكار
gift shop	maḥall hadāya (m)	محلّ هدايا
to take pictures	ṣawwar	صوّر
to have one's picture taken	taṣawwar	تصوّر

TRANSPORTATION

23. Airport

airport	maṭār (m)	مطار
airplane	ṭā'ira (f)	طائرة
airline	ʃarikat ṭayarān (f)	شركة طيران
air traffic controller	marāqib al ḥaraka al ʒawwiyya (pl)	مراقب الحركة الجوّية
departure	muɣādara (f)	مغادرة
arrival	wuṣūl (m)	وصول
to arrive (by plane)	waṣal	وصل
departure time	waqt al muɣādara (m)	وقت المغادرة
arrival time	waqt al wuṣūl (m)	وقت الوصول
to be delayed	ta'aχχar	تأخّر
flight delay	ta'aχχur ar riḥla (m)	تأخّر الرحلة
information board	lawḥat al ma'lūmāt (f)	لوحة المعلومات
information	isti'lāmāt (pl)	إستعلامات
to announce (vt)	a'lan	أعلن
flight (e.g., next ~)	riḥla (f)	رحلة
customs	ʒamārik (pl)	جمارك
customs officer	muwazzaf al ʒamārik (m)	موظّف الجمارك
customs declaration	taṣrīḥ ʒumrukiy (m)	تصريح جمركيّ
to fill out (vt)	mala'	ملأ
to fill out the declaration	mala' at taṣrīḥ	ملأ التصريح
passport control	taftīʃ al ʒawāzāt (m)	تفتيش الجوازات
luggage	aʃ ʃunaṭ (pl)	الشنط
hand luggage	ʃunaṭ al yad (pl)	شنط اليد
luggage cart	'arabat ʃunaṭ (f)	عربة شنط
landing	hubūṭ (m)	هبوط
landing strip	mamarr al hubūṭ (m)	ممرّ الهبوط
to land (vi)	habaṭ	هبط
airstairs	sullam aṭ ṭā'ira (m)	سلّم الطائرة
check-in	tasʒīl (m)	تسجيل
check-in counter	makān at tasʒīl (m)	مكان التسجيل
to check-in (vi)	saʒʒal	سجّل
boarding pass	biṭāqat ṣu'ūd (f)	بطاقة صعود

departure gate	bawwābat al muɣādara (f)	بوّابة المغادرة
transit	tranzīt (m)	ترانزيت
to wait (vt)	intazar	إنتظر
departure lounge	qā'at al muɣādara (f)	قاعة المغادرة
to see off	waddaʿ	ودّع
to say goodbye	waddaʿ	ودّع

24. Airplane

airplane	tā'ira (f)	طائرة
air ticket	taðkirat tā'ira (f)	تذكرة طائرة
airline	ʃarikat tayarān (f)	شركة طيران
airport	matār (m)	مطار
supersonic (adj)	xāriq liş şawt	خارق للصوت
captain	qā'id at tā'ira (m)	قائد الطائرة
crew	tāqim (m)	طاقم
pilot	tayyār (m)	طيّار
flight attendant (fem.)	mudīfat tayarān (f)	مضيفة طيران
navigator	mallāḥ (m)	ملّاح
wings	aʒniḥa (pl)	أجنحة
tail	ðayl (m)	ذيل
cockpit	kabīna (f)	كابينة
engine	mutūr (m)	موتور
undercarriage (landing gear)	'aʒalāt al hubūt (pl)	عجلات الهبوط
turbine	turbīna (f)	تربينة
propeller	mirwaḥa (f)	مروحة
black box	musaʒʒil at tayarān (m)	مسجّل الطيران
yoke (control column)	'aʒalat qiyāda (f)	عجلة قيادة
fuel	wuqūd (m)	وقود
safety card	bitāqat as salāma (f)	بطاقة السلامة
oxygen mask	qinā' uksiʒīn (m)	قناع أوكسيجين
uniform	libās muwaḥḥad (m)	لباس موحّد
life vest	sutrat naʒāt (f)	سترة نجاة
parachute	mizallat hubūt (f)	مظلّة هبوط
takeoff	iqlāʿ (m)	إقلاع
to take off (vi)	aqla'at	أقلعت
runway	madraʒ at tā'irāt (m)	مدرج الطائرات
visibility	ru'ya (f)	رؤية
flight (act of flying)	tayarān (m)	طيران
altitude	irtifāʿ (m)	إرتفاع
air pocket	ʒayb hawā'iy (m)	جيب هوائيّ
seat	maq'ad (m)	مقعد
headphones	sammā'āt ra'siya (pl)	سمّاعات رأسيّة

folding tray (tray table)	şīniyya qābila liṭ ṭayy (f)	صينية قابلة للطيّ
airplane window	ʃubbāk aṭ ṭā'ira (m)	شبّاك الطائرة
aisle	mamarr (m)	ممرّ

25. Train

train	qiṭār (m)	قطار
commuter train	qiṭār (m)	قطار
express train	qiṭār sarīʻ (m)	قطار سريع
diesel locomotive	qāṭirat dīzil (f)	قاطرة ديزل
steam locomotive	qāṭira buxāriyya (f)	قاطرة بخاريّة

| passenger car | ʻaraba (f) | عربة |
| dining car | ʻarabat al maṭʻam (f) | عربة المطعم |

rails	quḍubān (pl)	قضبان
railroad	sikka ḥadīdiyya (f)	سكّة حديديّة
railway tie	ʻāriḍa (f)	عارضة

platform (railway ~)	raṣīf (m)	رصيف
track (~ 1, 2, etc.)	xaṭṭ (m)	خطّ
semaphore	simafūr (m)	سيمافور
station	maḥaṭṭa (f)	محطّة

engineer (train driver)	sā'iq (m)	سائق
porter (of luggage)	ḥammāl (m)	حمّال
car attendant	mas'ūl ʻarabat al qiṭār (m)	مسؤول عربة القطار
passenger	rākib (m)	راكب
conductor (ticket inspector)	kamsariy (m)	كمسريّ

| corridor (in train) | mamarr (m) | ممرّ |
| emergency brake | farāmil aṭ ṭawāri' (pl) | فرامل الطوارئ |

compartment	ɣurfa (f)	غرفة
berth	sarīr (m)	سرير
upper berth	sarīr ʻulwiy (m)	سرير علويّ
lower berth	sarīr sufliy (m)	سرير سفليّ
bed linen, bedding	aɣṭiyat as sarīr (pl)	أغطية السرير

ticket	taðkira (f)	تذكرة
schedule	ʒadwal (m)	جدول
information display	lawḥat maʻlūmāt (f)	لوحة معلومات

to leave, to depart	ɣādar	غادر
departure (of train)	muɣādara (f)	مغادرة
to arrive (ab. train)	waṣal	وصل
arrival	wuṣūl (m)	وصول
to arrive by train	waṣal bil qiṭār	وصل بالقطار
to get on the train	rakib al qiṭār	ركب القطار

to get off the train	nazil min al qiṭār	نزل من القطار
train wreck	ḥiṭām qiṭār (m)	حطام قطار
to derail (vi)	xaraʒ ʿan xaṭṭ sayrih	خرج عن خطّ سيره
steam locomotive	qāṭira buxāriyya (f)	قاطرة بخاريّة
stoker, fireman	ʾataʃʒiy (m)	عطشجي
firebox	furn al muḥarrik (m)	فرن المحرّك
coal	faḥm (m)	فحم

26. Ship

ship	safīna (f)	سفينة
vessel	safīna (f)	سفينة
steamship	bāxira (f)	باخرة
riverboat	bāxira nahriyya (f)	باخرة نهريّة
cruise ship	bāxira siyahiyya (f)	باخرة سياحيّة
cruiser	ṭarrād (m)	طرّاد
yacht	yaxt (m)	يخت
tugboat	qāṭira (f)	قاطرة
barge	ṣandal (m)	صندل
ferry	ʿabbāra (f)	عبّارة
sailing ship	safīna ʃirāʿiyya (m)	سفينة شراعيّة
brigantine	markab ʃirāʿiy (m)	مركب شراعيّ
ice breaker	muḥaṭṭimat ʒalīd (f)	محطّمة جليد
submarine	ɣawwāṣa (f)	غوّاصة
boat (flat-bottomed ~)	markab (m)	مركب
dinghy	zawraq (m)	زورق
lifeboat	qārib naʒāt (m)	قارب نجاة
motorboat	lanʃ (m)	لنش
captain	qubṭān (m)	قبطان
seaman	baḥḥār (m)	بحّار
sailor	baḥḥār (m)	بحّار
crew	ṭāqim (m)	طاقم
boatswain	raʾīs al baḥḥāra (m)	رئيس البحّارة
ship's boy	ṣabiy as safīna (m)	صبي السفينة
cook	ṭabbāx (m)	طبّاخ
ship's doctor	ṭabīb as safīna (m)	طبيب السفينة
deck	saṭḥ as safīna (m)	سطح السفينة
mast	sāriya (f)	سارية
sail	ʃirāʿ (m)	شراع
hold	ʿambar (m)	عنبر
bow (prow)	muqaddama (f)	مقدّمة

stern	mu'axirat as safīna (f)	مؤخرة السفينة
oar	miʒðāf (m)	مجذاف
screw propeller	mirwaḥa (f)	مروحة
cabin	kabīna (f)	كابينة
wardroom	ɣurfat al istirāḥa (f)	غرفة الإستراحة
engine room	qism al 'ālāt (m)	قسم الآلات
bridge	burʒ al qiyāda (m)	برج القيادة
radio room	ɣurfat al lāsilkiy (f)	غرفة اللاسلكيّ
wave (radio)	mawʒa (f)	موجة
logbook	siʒil as safīna (m)	سجل السفينة
spyglass	minẓār (m)	منظار
bell	ʒaras (m)	جرس
flag	ʿalam (m)	علم
hawser (mooring ~)	ḥabl (m)	حبل
knot (bowline, etc.)	ʿuqda (f)	عقدة
deckrails	drabizīn (m)	درابزين
gangway	sullam (m)	سلّم
anchor	mirsāt (f)	مرساة
to weigh anchor	rafaʿ mirsāt	رفع مرساة
to drop anchor	rasa	رسا
anchor chain	silsilat mirsāt (f)	سلسلة مرساة
port (harbor)	mīnā' (m)	ميناء
quay, wharf	marsa (m)	مرسى
to berth (moor)	rasa	رسا
to cast off	aqlaʿ	أقلع
trip, voyage	riḥla (f)	رحلة
cruise (sea trip)	riḥla baḥriyya (f)	رحلة بحرية
course (route)	masār (m)	مسار
route (itinerary)	ṭarīq (m)	طريق
fairway (safe water channel)	maʒra milāḥiy (m)	مجرى ملاحيّ
shallows	miyāh ḍaḥla (f)	مياه ضحلة
to run aground	ʒanaḥ	جنح
storm	ʿāṣifa (f)	عاصفة
signal	iʃāra (f)	إشارة
to sink (vi)	ɣariq	غرق
Man overboard!	saqaṭ raʒul min as safīna!	سقط رجل من السفينة!
SOS (distress signal)	nidā' iɣāθa (m)	نداء إغاثة
ring buoy	ṭawq naʒāt (m)	طوق نجاة

CITY

27. Urban transportation

bus	bāṣ (m)	باص
streetcar	trām (m)	ترام
trolley bus	truli bāṣ (m)	ترولي باص
route (of bus, etc.)	xaṭṭ (m)	خط
number (e.g., bus ~)	raqm (m)	رقم
to go by ...	rakib ...	ركب...
to get on (~ the bus)	rakib	ركب
to get off ...	nazil min	نزل من
stop (e.g., bus ~)	mawqif (m)	موقف
next stop	al maḥaṭṭa al qādima (f)	المحطة القادمة
terminus	āxir maḥaṭṭa (f)	آخر محطة
schedule	ʒadwal (m)	جدول
to wait (vt)	intaẓar	إنتظر
ticket	taðkira (f)	تذكرة
fare	uʒra (f)	أجرة
cashier (ticket seller)	ṣarrāf (m)	صرّاف
ticket inspection	taftīʃ taðkira (m)	تفتيش تذكرة
ticket inspector	mufattiʃ taðākir (m)	مفتش تذاكر
to be late (for ...)	taʼaxxar	تأخّر
to miss (~ the train, etc.)	taʼaxxar	تأخّر
to be in a hurry	istaʻʒal	إستعجل
taxi, cab	taksi (m)	تاكسي
taxi driver	sāʼiq taksi (m)	سائق تاكسي
by taxi	bit taksi	بالتاكسي
taxi stand	mawqif taksi (m)	موقف تاكسي
to call a taxi	kallam tāksi	كلّم تاكسي
to take a taxi	axað taksi	أخذ تاكسي
traffic	ḥarakat al murūr (f)	حركة المرور
traffic jam	zaḥmat al murūr (f)	زحمة المرور
rush hour	sāʼat að ðurwa (f)	ساعة الذروة
to park (vi)	awqaf	أوقف
to park (vt)	awqaf	أوقف
parking lot	mawqif as sayyārāt (m)	موقف السيارات
subway	mitru (m)	مترو
station	maḥaṭṭa (f)	محطة

to take the subway	rakib al mitru	ركب المترو
train	qiṭār (m)	قطار
train station	maḥaṭṭat qiṭār (f)	محطّة قطار

28. City. Life in the city

city, town	madīna (f)	مدينة
capital city	ʿāṣima (f)	عاصمة
village	qarya (f)	قرية

city map	xarīṭat al madīna (f)	خريطة المدينة
downtown	markaz al madīna (m)	مركز المدينة
suburb	ḍāḥiya (f)	ضاحية
suburban (adj)	aḍ ḍawāḥi	الضواحي

outskirts	aṭrāf al madīna (pl)	أطراف المدينة
environs (suburbs)	ḍawāḥi al madīna (pl)	ضواحي المدينة
city block	ḥayy (m)	حيّ
residential block (area)	ḥayy sakaniy (m)	حيّ سكني

traffic	ḥarakat al murūr (f)	حركة المرور
traffic lights	iʃārāt al murūr (pl)	إشارات المرور
public transportation	wasāʾil an naql (pl)	وسائل النقل
intersection	taqāṭuʿ (m)	تقاطع

crosswalk	maʿbar al muʃāt (m)	معبر المشاة
pedestrian underpass	nafaq muʃāt (m)	نفق مشاة
to cross (~ the street)	ʿabar	عبر
pedestrian	māʃi (m)	ماش
sidewalk	raṣīf (m)	رصيف

bridge	ʒisr (m)	جسر
embankment (river walk)	kurnīʃ (m)	كورنيش
fountain	nāfūra (f)	نافورة

allée (garden walkway)	mamʃa (m)	ممشى
park	ḥadīqa (f)	حديقة
boulevard	bulvār (m)	بولفار
square	maydān (m)	ميدان
avenue (wide street)	ʃāriʿ (m)	شارع
street	ʃāriʿ (m)	شارع
side street	zuqāq (m)	زقاق
dead end	ṭarīq masdūd (m)	طريق مسدود

house	bayt (m)	بيت
building	mabna (m)	مبنى
skyscraper	nāṭiḥat saḥāb (f)	ناطحة سحاب

| facade | wāʒiha (f) | واجهة |
| roof | saqf (m) | سقف |

window	ʃubbāk (m)	شبّاك
arch	qaws (m)	قوس
column	'amūd (m)	عمود
corner	zāwiya (f)	زاوية
store window	vatrīna (f)	فترينة
signboard (store sign, etc.)	lāfita (f)	لافتة
poster	mulṣaq (m)	ملصق
advertising poster	mulṣaq i'lāniy (m)	ملصق إعلاني
billboard	lawḥat i'lānāt (f)	لوحة إعلانات
garbage, trash	zubāla (f)	زبالة
trashcan (public ~)	ṣundūq zubāla (m)	صندوق زبالة
to litter (vi)	rama zubāla	رمى زبالة
garbage dump	mazbala (f)	مزبلة
phone booth	kuʃk tilifūn (m)	كشك تليفون
lamppost	'amūd al miṣbāḥ (m)	عمود المصباح
bench (park ~)	dikka (f), kursiy (m)	دكّة, كرسي
police officer	ʃurṭiy (m)	شرطيّ
police	ʃurṭa (f)	شرطة
beggar	ʃaḥḥāð (m)	شحّاذ
homeless (n)	mutaʃarrid (m)	متشرّد

29. Urban institutions

store	maḥall (m)	محلّ
drugstore, pharmacy	ṣaydaliyya (f)	صيدليّة
eyeglass store	al adawāt al baṣariyya (pl)	الأدوات البصريّة
shopping mall	markaz tiȝāriy (m)	مركز تجاريّ
supermarket	subirmarkit (m)	سوبرماركت
bakery	maxbaz (m)	مخبز
baker	xabbāz (m)	خبّاز
pastry shop	dukkān ḥalawāniy (m)	دكّان حلوانيّ
grocery store	baqqāla (f)	بقّالة
butcher shop	malḥama (f)	ملحمة
produce store	dukkān xuḍār (m)	دكّان خضار
market	sūq (f)	سوق
coffee house	kafé (m), maqha (m)	كافيه, مقهى
restaurant	maṭ'am (m)	مطعم
pub, bar	ḥāna (f)	حانة
pizzeria	maṭ'am pizza (m)	مطعم بيتزا
hair salon	ṣālūn ḥilāqa (m)	صالون حلاقة
post office	maktab al barīd (m)	مكتب البريد
dry cleaners	tanȝīf ȝaff (m)	تنظيف جافّ

photo studio	istūdiyu taṣwīr (m)	إستوديو تصوير
shoe store	maḥall aḥðiya (m)	محلّ أحذية
bookstore	maḥall kutub (m)	محلّ كتب
sporting goods store	maḥall riyāḍiy (m)	محلّ رياضيّ
clothes repair shop	maḥall xiyāṭat malābis (m)	محلّ خياطة ملابس
formal wear rental	maḥall ta'ʒīr malābis rasmiyya (m)	محلّ تأجير ملابس رسمية
video rental store	maḥal ta'ʒīr vidiyu (m)	محلّ تأجير فيديو
circus	sirk (m)	سيرك
zoo	ḥadīqat al ḥayawān (f)	حديقة حيوان
movie theater	sinima (f)	سينما
museum	matḥaf (m)	متحف
library	maktaba (f)	مكتبة
theater	masraḥ (m)	مسرح
opera (opera house)	ubra (f)	أوبرا
nightclub	malha layliy (m)	ملهى ليليّ
casino	kazinu (m)	كازينو
mosque	masʒid (m)	مسجد
synagogue	kanīs ma'bad yahūdiy (m)	كنيس معبد يهوديّ
cathedral	katidrā'iyya (f)	كاتدرائيّة
temple	ma'bad (m)	معبد
church	kanīsa (f)	كنيسة
college	kulliyya (m)	كلّيّة
university	ʒāmi'a (f)	جامعة
school	madrasa (f)	مدرسة
prefecture	muqāṭa'a (f)	مقاطعة
city hall	baladiyya (f)	بلديّة
hotel	funduq (m)	فندق
bank	bank (m)	بنك
embassy	safāra (f)	سفارة
travel agency	ʃarikat siyāḥa (f)	شركة سياحة
information office	maktab al isti'lāmāt (m)	مكتب الإستعلامات
currency exchange	ṣarrāfa (f)	صرّافة
subway	mitru (m)	مترو
hospital	mustaʃfa (m)	مستشفى
gas station	maḥaṭṭat banzīn (f)	محطّة بنزين
parking lot	mawqif as sayyārāt (m)	موقف السيّارات

30. Signs

signboard (store sign, etc.)	lāfita (f)	لافتة
notice (door sign, etc.)	bayān (m)	بيان

poster	mulṣaq i'lāniy (m)	ملصق إعلانيّ
direction sign	'alāmat ittiʒāh (f)	علامة إتّجاه
arrow (sign)	'alāmat iʃāra (f)	علامة إشارة
caution	taḥðīr (m)	تحذير
warning sign	lāfitat taḥðīr (f)	لافتة تحذير
to warn (vt)	ḥaððar	حذَر
rest day (weekly ~)	yawm 'uṭla (m)	يوم عطلة
timetable (schedule)	ʒadwal (m)	جدول
opening hours	awqāt al 'amal (pl)	أوقات العمل
WELCOME!	ahlan wa sahlan!	أهلًا وسهلًا
ENTRANCE	duxūl	دخول
EXIT	xurūʒ	خروج
PUSH	idfa'	إدفع
PULL	isḥab	إسحب
OPEN	maftūḥ	مفتوح
CLOSED	muɣlaq	مغلق
WOMEN	lis sayyidāt	للسيدات
MEN	lir riʒāl	للرجال
DISCOUNTS	xaṣm	خصم
SALE	taxfīḍāt	تخفيضات
NEW!	ʒadīd!	جديد!
FREE	maʒʒānan	مجّانًا
ATTENTION!	intibāh!	إنتباه!
NO VACANCIES	kull al amākin maḥʒūza	كل الأماكن محجوزة
RESERVED	maḥʒūz	محجوز
ADMINISTRATION	idāra	إدارة
STAFF ONLY	lil 'āmilīn faqaṭ	للعاملين فقط
BEWARE OF THE DOG!	iḥðar wuʒūd al kalb	إحذر وجود الكلب
NO SMOKING	mamnū' at tadxīn	ممنوع التدخين
DO NOT TOUCH!	'adam al lams	عدم اللمس
DANGEROUS	xaṭīr	خطير
DANGER	xaṭar	خطر
HIGH VOLTAGE	tayyār 'āli	تيّار عالي
NO SWIMMING!	as sibāḥa mamnū'a	السباحة ممنوعة
OUT OF ORDER	mu'aṭṭal	معطّل
FLAMMABLE	sarī' al iʃti'āl	سريع الإشتعال
FORBIDDEN	mamnū'	ممنوع
NO TRESPASSING!	mamnū' al murūr	ممنوع المرور
WET PAINT	iḥðar ṭilā' ɣayr ʒāff	إحذر طلاء غير جاف

31. Shopping

to buy (purchase)	iʃtara	إشترى
purchase	ʃay' (m)	شيء
to go shopping	iʃtara	إشترى
shopping	ʃubinɣ (m)	شوبينغ
to be open (ab. store)	maftūḥ	مفتوح
to be closed	muɣlaq	مغلق
footwear, shoes	aḥðiya (pl)	أحذية
clothes, clothing	malābis (pl)	ملابس
cosmetics	mawādd at taʒmīl (pl)	موادّ التجميل
food products	ma'kūlāt (pl)	مأكولات
gift, present	hadiyya (f)	هديّة
salesman	bā'i' (m)	بائع
saleswoman	bā'i'a (f)	بائعة
check out, cash desk	ṣundū' ad daf' (m)	صندوق الدفع
mirror	mir'āt (f)	مرآة
counter (store ~)	minḍada (f)	منضدة
fitting room	ɣurfat al qiyās (f)	غرفة القياس
to try on	ʒarrab	جرّب
to fit (ab. dress, etc.)	nāsab	ناسب
to like (I like …)	a'ʒab	أعجب
price	si'r (m)	سعر
price tag	tikit as si'r (m)	تيكت السعر
to cost (vt)	kallaf	كلّف
How much?	bikam?	بكم؟
discount	xaṣm (m)	خصم
inexpensive (adj)	ɣayr ɣāli	غير غال
cheap (adj)	raxīṣ	رخيص
expensive (adj)	ɣāli	غال
It's expensive	haða ɣāli	هذا غال
rental (n)	isti'ʒār (m)	إستئجار
to rent (~ a tuxedo)	ista'ʒar	إستأجر
credit (trade credit)	i'timān (m)	إئتمان
on credit (adv)	bid dayn	بالدين

CLOTHING & ACCESSORIES

32. Outerwear. Coats

clothes	malābis (pl)	ملابس
outerwear	malābis fawqāniyya (pl)	ملابس فوقانيّة
winter clothing	malābis ʃitawiyya (pl)	ملابس شتويّة
coat (overcoat)	miʻṭaf (m)	معطف
fur coat	miʻṭaf farw (m)	معطف فرو
fur jacket	ʒakīt farw (m)	جاكيت فرو
down coat	haʃiyyat rīʃ (m)	حشبة ريش
jacket (e.g., leather ~)	ʒākīt (m)	جاكيت
raincoat (trenchcoat, etc.)	miʻṭaf lil maṭar (m)	معطف للمطر
waterproof (adj)	ṣāmid lil mā'	صامد للماء

33. Men's & women's clothing

shirt (button shirt)	qamīṣ (m)	قميص
pants	banṭalūn (m)	بنطلون
jeans	ʒīnz (m)	جينز
suit jacket	sutra (f)	سترة
suit	badla (f)	بدلة
dress (frock)	fustān (m)	فستان
skirt	tannūra (f)	تنّورة
blouse	blūza (f)	بلوزة
knitted jacket (cardigan, etc.)	kardigān (m)	كارديجان
jacket (of woman's suit)	ʒākīt (m)	جاكيت
T-shirt	ti ʃirt (m)	تي شيرت
shorts (short trousers)	ʃūrt (m)	شورت
tracksuit	badlat at tadrīb (f)	بدلة التدريب
bathrobe	θawb hammām (m)	ثوب حمّام
pajamas	biʒāma (f)	بيجاما
sweater	bulūvir (m)	بلوفر
pullover	bulūvir (m)	بلوفر
vest	ṣudayriy (m)	صديريّ
tailcoat	badlat sahra (f)	بدلة سهرة
tuxedo	smūkin (m)	سموكن

uniform	zayy muwaḥḥad (m)	زي موحّد
workwear	θiyāb al ʿamal (m)	ثياب العمل
overalls	uvirūl (m)	اوفرول
coat (e.g., doctor's smock)	θawb (m)	ثوب

34. Clothing. Underwear

underwear	malābis dāχiliyya (pl)	ملابس داخليّة
boxers, briefs	sirwāl dāχiliy riʒāliy (m)	سروال داخلي رجاليّ
panties	sirwāl dāχiliy nisāʾiy (m)	سروال داخلي نسائيّ
undershirt (A-shirt)	qamīṣ bila aqmām (m)	قميص بلا أكمام
socks	ʒawārib (pl)	جوارب

nightgown	qamīṣ nawm (m)	قميص نوم
bra	ḥammālat ṣadr (f)	حمّالة صدر
knee highs (knee-high socks)	ʒawārib ṭawīla (pl)	جوارب طويلة
pantyhose	ʒawārib kulūn (pl)	جوارب كولون
stockings (thigh highs)	ʒawārib nisāʾiyya (pl)	جوارب نسائية
bathing suit	libās sibāḥa (m)	لباس سباحة

35. Headwear

hat	qubbaʿa (f)	قبّعة
fedora	burnayṭa (f)	برنيطة
baseball cap	kāb baysbūl (m)	كاب بيسبول
flatcap	qubbaʿa musaṭṭaḥa (f)	قبّعة مسطحة

beret	birīh (m)	بيريه
hood	ɣiṭāʾ (m)	غطاء
panama hat	qubbaʿat banāma (f)	قبّعة بناما
knit cap (knitted hat)	qubbāʿa maḥbūka (m)	قبّعة محبوكة

headscarf	ʔiʒārb (m)	إيشارب
women's hat	burnayṭa (f)	برنيطة
hard hat	χūða (f)	خوذة
garrison cap	kāb (m)	كاب
helmet	χūða (f)	خوذة

| derby | qubbaʿat dirbi (f) | قبّعة ديربي |
| top hat | qubbaʿa ʿāliya (f) | قبّعة عالية |

36. Footwear

| footwear | aḥðiya (pl) | أحذية |
| shoes (men's shoes) | ʒazma (f) | جزمة |

shoes (women's shoes)	ӡazma (f)	جزمة
boots (e.g., cowboy ~)	būt (m)	بوت
slippers	ʃibʃib (m)	شبشب
tennis shoes (e.g., Nike ~)	ḥiðā' riyāḍiy (m)	حذاء رياضيّ
sneakers (e.g., Converse ~)	kutʃi (m)	كوتشي
sandals	ṣandal (pl)	صندل
cobbler (shoe repairer)	iskāfiy (m)	إسكافيّ
heel	kaʿb (m)	كعب
pair (of shoes)	zawӡ (m)	زوج
shoestring	ʃarīṭ (m)	شريط
to lace (vt)	rabaṭ	ربط
shoehorn	labbāsat ḥiðā' (f)	لبّاسة حذاء
shoe polish	warnīʃ al ḥiðā' (m)	ورنيش الحذاء

37. Personal accessories

gloves	quffāz (m)	قفّاز
mittens	quffāz muɣlaq (m)	قفّاز مغلق
scarf (muffler)	ʃʃārb (m)	إيشارب
glasses (eyeglasses)	nazẓāra (f)	نظّارة
frame (eyeglass ~)	iṭār (m)	إطار
umbrella	ʃamsiyya (f)	شمسيّة
walking stick	ʿaṣa (f)	عصا
hairbrush	furʃat ʃaʿr (f)	فرشة شعر
fan	mirwaḥa yadawiyya (f)	مروحة يدويّة
tie (necktie)	karavatta (f)	كرافتة
bow tie	babyūn (m)	ببيون
suspenders	ḥammāla (f)	حمّالة
handkerchief	mandīl (m)	منديل
comb	miʃṭ (m)	مشط
barrette	dabbūs (m)	دبّوس
hairpin	bansa (m)	بنسة
buckle	bukla (f)	بكلة
belt	ḥizām (m)	حزام
shoulder strap	ḥammalat al katf (f)	حمّالة الكتف
bag (handbag)	ʃanṭa (f)	شنطة
purse	ʃanṭat yad (f)	شنطة يد
backpack	ḥaqībat ẓahr (f)	حقيبة ظهر

38. Clothing. Miscellaneous

fashion	mūḍa (f)	موضة
in vogue (adj)	fil mūḍa	في الموضة
fashion designer	muṣammim azyā' (m)	مصمّم أزياء
collar	yāqa (f)	ياقة
pocket	ʒayb (m)	جيب
pocket (as adj)	ʒayb	جيب
sleeve	kumm (m)	كمّ
hanging loop	'allāqa (f)	علّاقة
fly (on trousers)	lisān (m)	لسان
zipper (fastener)	zimām munzaliq (m)	زمام منزلق
fastener	miʃbak (m)	مشبك
button	zirr (m)	زرّ
buttonhole	'urwa (f)	عروة
to come off (ab. button)	waqa'	وقع
to sew (vi, vt)	xāṭ	خاط
to embroider (vi, vt)	ṭarraz	طرّز
embroidery	taṭrīz (m)	تطريز
sewing needle	ibra (f)	إبرة
thread	xayṭ (m)	خيط
seam	darz (m)	درز
to get dirty (vi)	tawassax	توسّخ
stain (mark, spot)	buq'a (f)	بقعة
to crease, crumple (vi)	takarmaʃ	تكرمش
to tear, to rip (vt)	qaṭṭa'	قطّع
clothes moth	'uθθa (f)	عثّة

39. Personal care. Cosmetics

toothpaste	ma'ʒūn asnān (m)	معجون أسنان
toothbrush	furʃat asnān (f)	فرشة أسنان
to brush one's teeth	naẓẓaf al asnān	نظّف الأسنان
razor	mūs ḥilāqa (m)	موس حلاقة
shaving cream	krīm ḥilāqa (m)	كريم حلاقة
to shave (vi)	ḥalaq	حلق
soap	ṣābūn (m)	صابون
shampoo	ʃāmbū (m)	شامبو
scissors	maqaṣṣ (m)	مقصّ
nail file	mibrad (m)	مبرد
nail clippers	milqaṭ (m)	ملقط
tweezers	milqaṭ (m)	ملقط

cosmetics	mawādd at taʒmīl (pl)	مواد التجميل
face mask	mask (m)	ماسك
manicure	manikūr (m)	مانيكور
to have a manicure	ʿamal manikūr	عمل مانيكور
pedicure	badikīr (m)	باديكير
make-up bag	ḥaqībat adawāt at taʒmīl (f)	حقيبة أدوات التجميل
face powder	budrat waʒh (f)	بودرة وجه
powder compact	ʿulbat būdra (f)	علبة بودرة
blusher	aḥmar xudūd (m)	أحمر خدود
perfume (bottled)	ʿiṭr (m)	عطر
toilet water (lotion)	kulūnya (f)	كولونيا
lotion	lusiyun (m)	لوسيون
cologne	kulūniya (f)	كولونيا
eyeshadow	ay ʃaduw (m)	اي شادو
eyeliner	kuḥl al ʿuyūn (m)	كحل العيون
mascara	maskara (f)	ماسكارا
lipstick	aḥmar ʃifāh (m)	أحمر شفاه
nail polish, enamel	mulammiʿ al aẓāfir (m)	ملمّع الاظافر
hair spray	muθabbit aʃ ʃaʿr (m)	مثبّت الشعر
deodorant	muzīl rawāʾiḥ (m)	مزيل روائح
cream	krīm (m)	كريم
face cream	krīm lil waʒh (m)	كريم للوجه
hand cream	krīm lil yadayn (m)	كريم لليدين
anti-wrinkle cream	krīm muḍādd lit taʒāʿīd (m)	كريم مضادّ للتجاعيد
day cream	krīm an nahār (m)	كريم النهار
night cream	krīm al layl (m)	كريم الليل
day (as adj)	nahāriy	نهاريّ
night (as adj)	layliy	ليلي
tampon	tambūn (m)	تانبون
toilet paper (toilet roll)	waraq ḥammām (m)	ورق حمّام
hair dryer	muʒaffif ʃaʿr (m)	مجفّف شعر

40. Watches. Clocks

watch (wristwatch)	sāʿa (f)	ساعة
dial	waʒh as sāʿa (m)	وجه الساعة
hand (of clock, watch)	ʿaqrab as sāʿa (m)	عقرب الساعة
metal watch band	siwār sāʿa maʿdaniyya (m)	سوار ساعة معدنية
watch strap	siwār sāʿa (m)	سوار ساعة
battery	baṭṭāriyya (f)	بطّاريّة
to be dead (battery)	tafarraɣ	تفرّغ
to change a battery	ɣayyar al baṭṭāriyya	غيّر البطّاريّة
to run fast	sabaq	سبق

to run slow	ta'axxar	تأخّر
wall clock	sā'at ḥā'iṭ (f)	ساعة حائط
hourglass	sā'a ramliyya (f)	ساعة رمليّة
sundial	sā'a ʃamsiyya (f)	ساعة شمسيّة
alarm clock	munabbih (m)	منبّه
watchmaker	sa'ātiy (m)	ساعاتيّ
to repair (vt)	aṣlaḥ	أصلح

EVERYDAY EXPERIENCE

41. Money

money	nuqūd (pl)	نقود
currency exchange	taḥwīl 'umla (m)	تحويل عملة
exchange rate	si'r aṣ ṣarf (m)	سعر الصرف
ATM	ṣarrāf 'āliy (m)	صرّاف آليّ
coin	qiṭ'a naqdiyya (f)	قطعة نقديّة
dollar	dulār (m)	دولار
euro	yuru (m)	يورو
lira	lira iṭāliyya (f)	ليرة إيطالية
Deutschmark	mark almāniy (m)	مارك ألماني
franc	frank (m)	فرنك
pound sterling	ʒunayh istirlīniy (m)	جنيه استرلينيّ
yen	yīn (m)	ين
debt	dayn (m)	دين
debtor	mudīn (m)	مدين
to lend (money)	sallaf	سلّف
to borrow (vi, vt)	istalaf	إستلف
bank	bank (m)	بنك
account	ḥisāb (m)	حساب
to deposit (vt)	awda'	أودع
to deposit into the account	awda' fil ḥisāb	أودع في الحساب
to withdraw (vt)	saḥab min al ḥisāb	سحب من الحساب
credit card	biṭāqat i'timān (f)	بطاقة إئتمان
cash	nuqūd (pl)	نقود
check	ʃīk (m)	شيك
to write a check	katab ʃīk	كتب شيكًا
checkbook	daftar ʃīkāt (m)	دفتر شيكات
wallet	maḥfaẓat ʒīb (f)	محفظة جيب
change purse	maḥfaẓat fakka (f)	محفظة فكّة
safe	xizāna (f)	خزانة
heir	wāris (m)	وارث
inheritance	wirāθa (f)	وراثة
fortune (wealth)	θarwa (f)	ثروة
lease	'īʒār (m)	إيجار
rent (money)	uʒrat as sakan (f)	أجرة السكن

to rent (sth from sb)	istaʾʒar	إستأجِر
price	siʿr (m)	سِعر
cost	θaman (m)	ثمن
sum	mablaɣ (m)	مبلغ

to spend (vt)	ṣaraf	صرف
expenses	maṣārīf (pl)	مصاريف
to economize (vi, vt)	waffar	وفّر
economical	muwaffir	موفّر

to pay (vi, vt)	dafaʿ	دفع
payment	dafʿ (m)	دفع
change (give the ~)	al bāqi (m)	الباقي

tax	ḍarība (f)	ضريبة
fine	ɣarāma (f)	غرامة
to fine (vt)	faraḍ ɣarāma	فرض غرامة

42. Post. Postal service

post office	maktab al barīd (m)	مكتب البريد
mail (letters, etc.)	al barīd (m)	البريد
mailman	sāʿi al barīd (m)	ساعي البريد
opening hours	awqāt al ʿamal (pl)	أوقات العمل

letter	risāla (f)	رسالة
registered letter	risāla musaʒʒala (f)	رسالة مسجّلة
postcard	biṭāqa barīdiyya (f)	بطاقة بريديّة
telegram	barqiyya (f)	برقيّة
package (parcel)	ṭard (m)	طرد
money transfer	ḥawāla māliyya (f)	حوالة ماليّة

to receive (vt)	istalam	إستلم
to send (vt)	arsal	أرسل
sending	irsāl (m)	إرسال

address	ʿunwān (m)	عنوان
ZIP code	raqm al barīd (m)	رقم البريد
sender	mursil (m)	مرسل
receiver	mursal ilayh (m)	مرسل إليه

| name (first name) | ism (m) | إسم |
| surname (last name) | ism al ʿāʾila (m) | إسم العائلة |

postage rate	taʿrīfa (f)	تعريفة
standard (adj)	ʿādiy	عاديّ
economical (adj)	muwaffir	موفّر

| weight | wazn (m) | وزن |
| to weigh (~ letters) | wazan | وزن |

envelope	ẓarf (m)	ظرف
postage stamp	ṭābi' (m)	طابع
to stamp an envelope	alṣaq ṭābi'	ألصق طابعا

43. Banking

| bank | bank (m) | بنك |
| branch (of bank, etc.) | far' (m) | فرع |

| bank clerk, consultant | muwaẓẓaf bank (m) | موظف بنك |
| manager (director) | mudīr (m) | مدير |

bank account	ḥisāb (m)	حساب
account number	raqm al ḥisāb (m)	رقم الحساب
checking account	ḥisāb ǧāri (m)	حساب جار
savings account	ḥisāb tawfīr (m)	حساب توفير

to open an account	fataḥ ḥisāb	فتح حسابا
to close the account	aɣlaq ḥisāb	أغلق حسابا
to deposit into the account	awda' fil ḥisāb	أودع في الحساب
to withdraw (vt)	saḥab min al ḥisāb	سحب من الحساب

| deposit | wadī'a (f) | وديعة |
| to make a deposit | awda' | أودع |

| wire transfer | ḥawāla (f) | حوالة |
| to wire, to transfer | ḥawwal | حوّل |

| sum | mablaɣ (m) | مبلغ |
| How much? | kam? | كم؟ |

| signature | tawqī' (m) | توقيع |
| to sign (vt) | waqqa' | وقّع |

| credit card | biṭāqat i'timān (f) | بطاقة ائتمان |
| code (PIN code) | kūd (m) | كود |

| credit card number | raqm biṭāqat i'timān (m) | رقم بطاقة إئتمان |
| ATM | ṣarrāf 'āliy (m) | صرّاف آليّ |

check	ʃīk (m)	شيك
to write a check	katab ʃīk	كتب شيكًا
checkbook	daftar ʃīkāt (m)	دفتر شيكات

loan (bank ~)	qarḍ (m)	قرض
to apply for a loan	qaddam ṭalab lil ḥuṣūl 'ala qarḍ	قدّم طلبا للحصول على قرض
to get a loan	ḥaṣal 'ala qarḍ	حصل على قرض
to give a loan	qaddam qarḍ	قدم قرضا
guarantee	ḍamān (m)	ضمان

44. Telephone. Phone conversation

telephone	hātif (m)	هاتف
cell phone	hātif maḥmūl (m)	هاتف محمول
answering machine	muʒīb al hātif (m)	مجيب الهاتف
to call (by phone)	ittaṣal	إتّصل
phone call	mukālama tilifuniyya (f)	مكالمة تليفونية
to dial a number	ittaṣal bi raqm	إتّصل برقم
Hello!	alu!	ألو!
to ask (vt)	sa'al	سأل
to answer (vi, vt)	radd	ردّ
to hear (vt)	samiʿ	سمع
well (adv)	ʒayyidan	جيّدًا
not well (adv)	sayyi'an	سيّئًا
noises (interference)	taʃwīʃ (m)	تشويش
receiver	sammāʿa (f)	سمّاعة
to pick up (~ the phone)	rafaʿ as sammāʿa	رفع السمّاعة
to hang up (~ the phone)	qafal as sammāʿa	قفل السمّاعة
busy (engaged)	maʃɣūl	مشغول
to ring (ab. phone)	rann	رنّ
telephone book	dalīl at tilifūn (m)	دليل التليفون
local (adj)	maḥalliyya	ة محلّيّة
local call	mukālama hātifiyya maḥalliyya (f)	مكالمة هاتفيّة محلّيّة
long distance (~ call)	baʿīd al mada	بعيد المدى
long-distance call	mukālama baʿīdat al mada (f)	مكالمة بعيدة المدى
international (adj)	duwaliy	دوليّ
international call	mukālama duwaliyya (f)	مكالمة دوليّة

45. Cell phone

cell phone	hātif maḥmūl (m)	هاتف محمول
display	ʒihāz ʿarḍ (m)	جهاز عرض
button	zirr (m)	زر
SIM card	sim kart (m)	سيم كارت
battery	baṭṭāriyya (f)	بطّاريّة
to be dead (battery)	xalaṣat	خلصت
charger	ʃāḥin (m)	شاحن
menu	qā'ima (f)	قائمة
settings	awḍāʿ (pl)	أوضاع

| tune (melody) | naɣma (f) | نغمة |
| to select (vt) | iχtār | إختار |

calculator	'āla ḥāsiba (f)	آلة حاسبة
voice mail	barīd ṣawtiy (m)	بريد صوتيّ
alarm clock	munabbih (m)	منبّه
contacts	ʒihāt al ittiṣāl (pl)	جهات الإتّصال

| SMS (text message) | risāla qaṣīra ɛsɛmɛs (f) | sms رسالة قصيرة |
| subscriber | muʃtarik (m) | مشترك |

46. Stationery

| ballpoint pen | qalam ʒāf (m) | قلم جاف |
| fountain pen | qalam rīʃa (m) | قلم ريشة |

pencil	qalam ruṣāṣ (m)	قلم رصاص
highlighter	markir (m)	ماركر
felt-tip pen	qalam χaṭṭāṭ (m)	قلم خطاط

| notepad | muðakkira (f) | مذكّرة |
| agenda (diary) | ʒadwal al a'māl (m) | جدول الأعمال |

ruler	masṭara (f)	مسطرة
calculator	'āla ḥāsiba (f)	آلة حاسبة
eraser	astīka (f)	استيكة
thumbtack	dabbūs (m)	دبّوس
paper clip	dabbūs waraq (m)	دبّوس ورق

glue	ṣamɣ (m)	صمغ
stapler	dabbāsa (f)	دبّاسة
hole punch	χarrāma (m)	خرّامة
pencil sharpener	mibrāt (f)	مبراة

47. Foreign languages

language	luɣa (f)	لغة
foreign (adj)	aʒnabiy	أجنبيّ
foreign language	luɣa aʒnabiyya (f)	لغة أجنبيّة
to study (vt)	daras	درس
to learn (language, etc.)	ta'allam	تعلّم

to read (vi, vt)	qara'	قرأ
to speak (vi, vt)	takallam	تكلّم
to understand (vt)	fahim	فهم
to write (vt)	katab	كتب
fast (adv)	bi sur'a	بسرعة
slowly (adv)	bi buṭ'	ببطء

fluently (adv)	bi ṭalāqa	بطلاقة
rules	qawā'id (pl)	قواعد
grammar	an naḥw waṣ ṣarf (m)	النحو والصرف
vocabulary	mufradāt al luɣa (pl)	مفردات اللغة
phonetics	ṣawtīyyāt (pl)	صوتيّات
textbook	kitāb taʿlīm (m)	كتاب تعليم
dictionary	qāmūs (m)	قاموس
teach-yourself book	kitāb taʿlīm ðātiy (m)	كتاب تعليم ذاتيّ
phrasebook	kitāb lil 'ibārāt aʃ ʃā'i'a (m)	كتاب للعبارت الشائعة
cassette, tape	ʃarīṭ (m)	شريط
videotape	ʃarīṭ vidiyu (m)	شريط فيديو
CD, compact disc	si di (m)	سي دي
DVD	di vi di (m)	دي في دي
alphabet	alifbā' (m)	الفباء
to spell (vt)	tahaʒʒa	تهجّى
pronunciation	nuṭq (m)	نطق
accent	lukna (f)	لكنة
with an accent	bi lukna	بلكنة
without an accent	bi dūn lukna	بدون لكنة
word	kalima (f)	كلمة
meaning	ma'na (m)	معنى
course (e.g., a French ~)	dawra (f)	دورة
to sign up	saʒʒal ismahu	سجّل إسمه
teacher	mudarris (m)	مدرّس
translation (process)	tarʒama (f)	ترجمة
translation (text, etc.)	tarʒama (f)	ترجمة
translator	mutarʒim (m)	مترجم
interpreter	mutarʒim fawriy (m)	مترجم فوريّ
polyglot	'alīm bi 'iddat luɣāt (m)	عليم بعدّة لغات
memory	ðākira (f)	ذاكرة

MEALS. RESTAURANT

48. Table setting

spoon	mil'aqa (f)	ملعقة
knife	sikkīn (m)	سكِّين
fork	ʃawka (f)	شوكة
cup (e.g., coffee ~)	finӡān (m)	فنجان
plate (dinner ~)	ṭabaq (m)	طبق
saucer	ṭabaq finӡān (m)	طبق فنجان
napkin (on table)	mandīl (m)	منديل
toothpick	χallat asnān (f)	خلّة أسنان

49. Restaurant

restaurant	maṭ'am (m)	مطعم
coffee house	kafé (m), maqha (m)	كافيه، مقهى
pub, bar	bār (m)	بار
tearoom	ṣālun ʃāy (m)	صالون شاي
waiter	nādil (m)	نادل
waitress	nādila (f)	نادلة
bartender	bārman (m)	بارمان
menu	qā'imat aṭ ṭa'ām (f)	قائمة طعام
wine list	qā'imat al χumūr (f)	قائمة خمور
to book a table	haӡaz mā'ida	حجز مائدة
course, dish	waӡba (f)	وجبة
to order (meal)	ṭalab	طلب
to make an order	ṭalab	طلب
aperitif	ʃarāb (m)	شراب
appetizer	muqabbilāt (pl)	مقبّلات
dessert	halawiyyāt (pl)	حلويَّات
check	hisāb (m)	حساب
to pay the check	dafa' al hisāb	دفع الحساب
to give change	a'ṭa al bāqi	أعطى الباقي
tip	baqʃiʃ (m)	بقشيش

50. Meals

| food | akl (m) | أكل |
| to eat (vi, vt) | akal | أكل |

breakfast	fuṭūr (m)	فطور
to have breakfast	afṭar	أفطر
lunch	ɣadā' (m)	غداء
to have lunch	taɣadda	تغدّى
dinner	'aʃā' (m)	عشاء
to have dinner	ta'aʃʃa	تعشّى

| appetite | ʃahiyya (f) | شهيّة |
| Enjoy your meal! | hanī'an marī'an! | هنيئًا مريئًا! |

to open (~ a bottle)	fataḥ	فتح
to spill (liquid)	dalaq	دلق
to spill out (vi)	indalaq	إندلق

to boil (vi)	ɣala	غلى
to boil (vt)	ɣala	غلى
boiled (~ water)	maɣliy	مغليّ
to chill, cool down (vt)	barrad	برّد
to chill (vi)	tabarrad	تبرّد

| taste, flavor | ṭa'm (m) | طعم |
| aftertaste | al maðāq al 'āliq fil fam (m) | المذاق العالق فى الفم |

to slim down (lose weight)	faqad al wazn	فقد الوزن
diet	ḥimya ɣaðā'iyya (f)	حمية غذائية
vitamin	vitamīn (m)	فيتامين
calorie	su'ra ḥarāriyya (f)	سعرة حراريّة
vegetarian (n)	nabātiy (m)	نباتيّ
vegetarian (adj)	nabātiy	نباتيّ

fats (nutrient)	duhūn (pl)	دهون
proteins	brutināt (pl)	بروتينات
carbohydrates	naʃawiyyāt (pl)	نشويّات
slice (of lemon, ham)	ʃarīḥa (f)	شريحة
piece (of cake, pie)	qiṭ'a (f)	قطعة
crumb (of bread, cake, etc.)	futāta (f)	فتاتة

51. Cooked dishes

course, dish	waʒba (f)	وجبة
cuisine	matbax (m)	مطبخ
recipe	waṣfa (f)	وصفة
portion	waʒba (f)	وجبة

salad	suḷṭa (f)	سلطة
soup	ʃūrba (f)	شوربة
clear soup (broth)	maraq (m)	مرق
sandwich (bread)	sandawitʃ (m)	ساندويتش
fried eggs	bayḍ maqliy (m)	بيض مقليّ
hamburger (beefburger)	hamburger (m)	هامبورجر
beefsteak	biftīk (m)	بفتيك
side dish	ṭabaq ʒānibiy (m)	طبق جانبيّ
spaghetti	spaɣitti (m)	سباغيتي
mashed potatoes	harīs baṭāṭis (m)	هريس بطاطس
pizza	bītza (f)	بيتزا
porridge (oatmeal, etc.)	ʿaṣīda (f)	عصيدة
omelet	bayḍ maxfūq (m)	بيض مخفوق
boiled (e.g., ~ beef)	maslūq	مسلوق
smoked (adj)	mudaxxin	مدخّن
fried (adj)	maqliy	مقليّ
dried (adj)	muʒaffaf	مجفّف
frozen (adj)	muʒammad	مجمّد
pickled (adj)	muxallil	مخلّل
sweet (sugary)	musakkar	مسكّر
salty (adj)	māliḥ	مالح
cold (adj)	bārid	بارد
hot (adj)	sāxin	ساخن
bitter (adj)	murr	مرّ
tasty (adj)	laðīð	لذيذ
to cook in boiling water	ṭabax	طبخ
to cook (dinner)	ḥaḍḍar	حضّر
to fry (vt)	qala	قلي
to heat up (food)	saxxan	سخّن
to salt (vt)	mallaḥ	ملّح
to pepper (vt)	falfal	فلفل
to grate (vt)	baʃar	بشر
peel (n)	qiʃra (f)	قشرة
to peel (vt)	qaʃʃar	قشّر

52. Food

meat	laḥm (m)	لحم
chicken	daʒāʒ (m)	دجاج
Rock Cornish hen (poussin)	farrūʒ (m)	فرّوج
duck	baṭṭa (f)	بطّة
goose	iwazza (f)	إوزّة

game	ṣayd (m)	صيد
turkey	daӡāӡ rūmiy (m)	دجاج رومي
pork	laḥm al xinzīr (m)	لحم الخنزير
veal	laḥm il ʻiӡl (m)	لحم العجل
lamb	laḥm aḍ ḍa'n (m)	لحم الضأن
beef	laḥm al baqar (m)	لحم البقر
rabbit	arnab (m)	أرنب
sausage (bologna, pepperoni, etc.)	suӡuq (m)	سجق
vienna sausage (frankfurter)	suӡuq (m)	سجق
bacon	bikūn (m)	بيكون
ham	hām (m)	هام
gammon	faxð xinzīr (m)	فخذ خنزير
pâté	ma'ӡūn laḥm (m)	معجون لحم
liver	kibda (f)	كبدة
hamburger (ground beef)	ḥaʃwa (f)	حشوة
tongue	lisān (m)	لسان
egg	bayḍa (f)	بيضة
eggs	bayḍ (m)	بيض
egg white	bayāḍ al bayḍ (m)	بياض البيض
egg yolk	ṣafār al bayḍ (m)	صفار البيض
fish	samak (m)	سمك
seafood	fawākih al baḥr (pl)	فواكه البحر
caviar	kaviyār (m)	كافيار
crab	salṭa'ūn (m)	سلطعون
shrimp	ӡambari (m)	جمبري
oyster	maḥār (m)	محار
spiny lobster	karkand ʃāik (m)	كركند شائك
octopus	uxṭubūṭ (m)	أخطبوط
squid	kalmāri (m)	كالماري
sturgeon	samak al ḥaʃʃ (m)	سمك الحفش
salmon	salmūn (m)	سلمون
halibut	samak al halbūt (m)	سمك الهلبوت
cod	samak al qudd (m)	سمك القدّ
mackerel	usqumriy (m)	أسقمريّ
tuna	tūna (f)	تونة
eel	ḥankalīs (m)	حنكليس
trout	salmūn muraqqaṭ (m)	سلمون مرقّط
sardine	sardīn (m)	سردين
pike	samak al karāki (m)	سمك الكراكي
herring	rinӡa (f)	رنجة
bread	xubz (m)	خبز

cheese	ʒubna (f)	جبنة
sugar	sukkar (m)	سكّر
salt	milḥ (m)	ملح
rice	urz (m)	أرز
pasta (macaroni)	makarūna (f)	مكرونة
noodles	nūdlis (f)	نودلز
butter	zubda (f)	زبدة
vegetable oil	zayt (m)	زيت
sunflower oil	zayt ʿabīd aʃ ʃams (m)	زيت عبيد الشمس
margarine	marɣarīn (m)	مرغرين
olives	zaytūn (m)	زيتون
olive oil	zayt az zaytūn (m)	زيت الزيتون
milk	ḥalīb (m)	حليب
condensed milk	ḥalīb mukaθθaf (m)	حليب مكثف
yogurt	yūɣurt (m)	يوغورت
sour cream	krīma ḥāmiḍa (f)	كريمة حامضة
cream (of milk)	krīma (f)	كريمة
mayonnaise	mayunīz (m)	مايونيز
buttercream	krīmat zubda (f)	كريمة زبدة
cereal grains (wheat, etc.)	ḥubūb (pl)	حبوب
flour	daqīq (m)	دقيق
canned food	muʿallabāt (pl)	معلبات
cornflakes	kurn fliks (m)	كورن فليكس
honey	ʿasal (m)	عسل
jam	murabba (m)	مربّى
chewing gum	ʿilk (m)	علك

53. Drinks

water	mā' (m)	ماء
drinking water	mā' ʃurb (m)	ماء شرب
mineral water	mā' maʿdaniy (m)	ماء معدنيّ
still (adj)	bi dūn ɣāz	بدون غاز
carbonated (adj)	mukarban	مكربن
sparkling (adj)	bil ɣāz	بالغاز
ice	θalʒ (m)	ثلج
with ice	biθ θalʒ	بالثلج
non-alcoholic (adj)	bi dūn kuḥūl	بدون كحول
soft drink	maʃrūb ɣāziy (m)	مشروب غازي
refreshing drink	maʃrūb muθallaʒ (m)	مشروب مثلج
lemonade	ʃarāb laymūn (m)	شراب ليمون

liquors	maʃrūbāt kuḥūliyya (pl)	مشروبات كحوليّة
wine	nabīð (f)	نبيذ
white wine	nibīð abyaḍ (m)	نبيذ أبيض
red wine	nabīð aḥmar (m)	نبيذ أحمر
liqueur	liqiūr (m)	ليكيور
champagne	ʃambāniya (f)	شمبانيا
vermouth	virmut (m)	فيرموث
whiskey	wiski (m)	وسكي
vodka	vudka (f)	فودكا
gin	ʒīn (m)	جين
cognac	kunyāk (m)	كونياك
rum	rum (m)	رم
coffee	qahwa (f)	قهوة
black coffee	qahwa sāda (f)	قهوة سادة
coffee with milk	qahwa bil ḥalīb (f)	قهوة بالحليب
cappuccino	kaputʃīnu (m)	كابتشينو
instant coffee	niskafi (m)	نيسكافيه
milk	ḥalīb (m)	حليب
cocktail	kuktayl (m)	كوكتيل
milkshake	milk ʃiyk (m)	ميلك شيك
juice	ʿaṣīr (m)	عصير
tomato juice	ʿaṣīr ṭamāṭim (m)	عصير طماطم
orange juice	ʿaṣīr burtuqāl (m)	عصير برتقال
freshly squeezed juice	ʿaṣīr ṭāziʒ (m)	عصير طازج
beer	bīra (f)	بيرة
light beer	bīra xafīfa (f)	بيرة خفيفة
dark beer	bīra ɣāmiqa (f)	بيرة غامقة
tea	ʃāy (m)	شاي
black tea	ʃāy aswad (m)	شاي أسود
green tea	ʃāy axḍar (m)	شاي أخضر

54. Vegetables

vegetables	xuḍār (pl)	خضار
greens	xuḍrawāt waraqiyya (pl)	خضروات ورقيّة
tomato	ṭamāṭim (f)	طماطم
cucumber	xiyār (m)	خيار
carrot	ʒazar (m)	جزر
potato	baṭāṭis (f)	بطاطس
onion	baṣal (m)	بصل
garlic	θūm (m)	ثوم
cabbage	kurumb (m)	كرنب

cauliflower	qarnabīṭ (m)	قرنبيط
Brussels sprouts	kurumb brūksil (m)	كرنب بروكسل
broccoli	brukuli (m)	بركولي

beetroot	banʒar (m)	بنجر
eggplant	bātinʒān (m)	باذنجان
zucchini	kūsa (f)	كوسة
pumpkin	qarʿ (m)	قرع
turnip	lift (m)	لفت

parsley	baqdūnis (m)	بقدونس
dill	ʃabat (m)	شبت
lettuce	xass (m)	خسّ
celery	karafs (m)	كرفس
asparagus	halyūn (m)	هليون
spinach	sabānix (m)	سبانخ

pea	bisilla (f)	بسلّة
beans	fūl (m)	فول
corn (maize)	ðura (f)	ذرّة
kidney bean	faṣūliya (f)	فاصوليا

bell pepper	filfil (m)	فلفل
radish	fiʒl (m)	فجل
artichoke	xurʃūf (m)	خرشوف

55. Fruits. Nuts

fruit	fākiha (f)	فاكهة
apple	tuffāḥa (f)	تفّاحة
pear	kummaθra (f)	كمّثرى
lemon	laymūn (m)	ليمون
orange	burtuqāl (m)	برتقال
strawberry (garden ~)	farawla (f)	فراولة

mandarin	yūsufiy (m)	يوسفي
plum	barqūq (m)	برقوق
peach	durrāq (m)	دراق
apricot	miʃmiʃ (f)	مشمش
raspberry	tūt al ʿullayq al aḥmar (m)	توت العلّيق الأحمر
pineapple	ananās (m)	أناناس

banana	mawz (m)	موز
watermelon	baṭṭīx aḥmar (m)	بطّيخ أحمر
grape	ʿinab (m)	عنب
cherry	karaz (m)	كرز
melon	baṭṭīx aṣfar (f)	بطّيخ أصفر

| grapefruit | zinbāʿ (m) | زنباع |
| avocado | avukādu (f) | افوكاتو |

papaya	babāya (m)	ببايا
mango	mangu (m)	مانجو
pomegranate	rummān (m)	رمان
redcurrant	kiʃmiʃ aḥmar (m)	كشمش أحمر
blackcurrant	'inab aθ θa'lab al aswad (m)	عنب الثعلب الأسود
gooseberry	'inab aθ θa'lab (m)	عنب الثعلب
bilberry	'inab al aḥrāʒ (m)	عنب الأحراج
blackberry	θamar al 'ullayk (m)	ثمر العليّق
raisin	zabīb (m)	زبيب
fig	tīn (m)	تين
date	tamr (m)	تمر
peanut	fūl sudāniy (m)	فول سودانيّ
almond	lawz (m)	لوز
walnut	'ayn al ʒamal (f)	عين الجمل
hazelnut	bunduq (m)	بندق
coconut	ʒawz al hind (m)	جوز هند
pistachios	fustuq (m)	فستق

56. Bread. Candy

bakers' confectionery (pastry)	ḥalawiyyāt (pl)	حلويّات
bread	xubz (m)	خبز
cookies	baskawīt (m)	بسكويت
chocolate (n)	ʃukulāta (f)	شكولاتة
chocolate (as adj)	biʃ ʃukulāta	بالشكولاتة
candy (wrapped)	bumbūn (m)	بونبون
cake (e.g., cupcake)	ka'k (m)	كعك
cake (e.g., birthday ~)	tūrta (f)	تورتة
pie (e.g., apple ~)	fatīra (f)	فطيرة
filling (for cake, pie)	ḥaʃwa (f)	حشوة
jam (whole fruit jam)	murabba (m)	مربّى
marmalade	marmalād (f)	مرملاد
waffles	wāfil (m)	وافل
ice-cream	muθallaʒāt (pl)	مثلّجات
pudding	būding (m)	بودنج

57. Spices

salt	milḥ (m)	ملح
salty (adj)	māliḥ	مالح

to salt (vt)	mallaḥ	ملّح
black pepper	filfil aswad (m)	فلفل أسود
red pepper (milled ~)	filfil aḥmar (m)	فلفل أحمر
mustard	ṣalṣat al χardal (f)	صلصة الخردل
horseradish	fiʒl ḥārr (m)	فجل حارّ
condiment	tābil (m)	تابل
spice	bahār (m)	بهار
sauce	ṣalṣa (f)	صلصة
vinegar	χall (m)	خلّ
anise	yānsūn (m)	يانسون
basil	rīḥān (m)	ريحان
cloves	qurumful (m)	قرنفل
ginger	zanʒabīl (m)	زنجبيل
coriander	kuzbara (f)	كزبرة
cinnamon	qirfa (f)	قرفة
sesame	simsim (m)	سمسم
bay leaf	awrāq al χār (pl)	أوراق الغار
paprika	babrika (f)	بابريكا
caraway	karāwiya (f)	كراوية
saffron	zaʿfarān (m)	زعفران

PERSONAL INFORMATION. FAMILY

58. Personal information. Forms

name (first name)	ism (m)	إسم
surname (last name)	ism al 'ā'ila (m)	إسم العائلة
date of birth	tarīχ al mīlād (m)	تاريخ الميلاد
place of birth	makān al mīlād (m)	مكان الميلاد
nationality	ʒinsiyya (f)	جنسية
place of residence	maqarr al iqāma (m)	مقر الإقامة
country	balad (m)	بلد
profession (occupation)	mihna (f)	مهنة
gender, sex	ʒins (m)	جنس
height	ṭūl (m)	طول
weight	wazn (m)	وزن

59. Family members. Relatives

mother	umm (f)	أُمّ
father	ab (m)	أب
son	ibn (m)	إبن
daughter	ibna (f)	إبنة
younger daughter	al ibna aṣ ṣaγīra (f)	الإبنة الصغيرة
younger son	al ibn aṣ ṣaγīr (m)	الابن الصغير
eldest daughter	al ibna al kabīra (f)	الإبنة الكبيرة
eldest son	al ibn al kabīr (m)	الإبن الكبير
brother	aχ (m)	أخ
elder brother	al aχ al kabīr (m)	الأخ الكبير
younger brother	al aχ aṣ ṣaγīr (m)	الأخ الصغير
sister	uχt (f)	أخت
elder sister	al uχt al kabīra (f)	الأخت الكبيرة
younger sister	al uχt aṣ ṣaγīra (f)	الأخت الصغيرة
cousin (masc.)	ibn 'amm (m), ibn χāl (m)	إبن عمّ، إبن خال
cousin (fem.)	ibnat 'amm (f), ibnat χāl (f)	إبنة عمّ، إبنة خال
mom, mommy	mama (f)	ماما
dad, daddy	baba (m)	بابا
parents	wālidān (du)	والدان
child	ṭifl (m)	طفل
children	aṭfāl (pl)	أطفال

grandmother	ʒidda (f)	جدّة
grandfather	ʒadd (m)	جدّ
grandson	ḥafīd (m)	حفيد
granddaughter	ḥafīda (f)	حفيدة
grandchildren	aḥfād (pl)	أحفاد

uncle	'amm (m), χāl (m)	عمّ, خال
aunt	'amma (f), χāla (f)	عمّة, خالة
nephew	ibn al aχ (m), ibn al uχt (m)	إبن الأخ, إبن الأخت
niece	ibnat al aχ (f), ibnat al uχt (f)	إبنة الأخ, إبنة الأخت
mother-in-law (wife's mother)	ḥamātt (f)	حماة
father-in-law (husband's father)	ḥamm (m)	حم
son-in-law (daughter's husband)	zawʒ al ibna (m)	زوج الأبنة
stepmother	zawʒat al ab (f)	زوجة الأب
stepfather	zawʒ al umm (m)	زوج الأمّ

infant	ṭifl raḍī' (m)	طفل رضيع
baby (infant)	mawlūd (m)	مولود
little boy, kid	walad ṣaɣīr (m)	ولد صغير

wife	zawʒa (f)	زوجة
husband	zawʒ (m)	زوج
spouse (husband)	zawʒ (m)	زوج
spouse (wife)	zawʒa (f)	زوجة

married (masc.)	mutazawwiʒ	متزوّج
married (fem.)	mutazawwiʒa	متزوّجة
single (unmarried)	a'zab	أعزب
bachelor	a'zab (m)	أعزب
divorced (masc.)	muṭallaq (m)	مطلّق
widow	armala (f)	أرملة
widower	armal (m)	أرمل

relative	qarīb (m)	قريب
close relative	nasīb qarīb (m)	نسيب قريب
distant relative	nasīb ba'īd (m)	نسيب بعيد
relatives	aqārib (pl)	أقارب

orphan (boy or girl)	yatīm (m)	يتيم
guardian (of a minor)	waliyy amr (m)	وليّ أمر
to adopt (a boy)	tabanna	تبنّى
to adopt (a girl)	tabanna	تبنّى

60. Friends. Coworkers

| friend (masc.) | ṣadīq (m) | صديق |
| friend (fem.) | ṣadīqa (f) | صديقة |

friendship	ṣadāqa (f)	صداقة
to be friends	ṣādaq	صادق
buddy (masc.)	ṣāḥib (m)	صاحب
buddy (fem.)	ṣaḥiba (f)	صاحبة
partner	rafīq (m)	رفيق
chief (boss)	raʾīs (m)	رئيس
superior (n)	raʾīs (m)	رئيس
owner, proprietor	ṣāḥib (m)	صاحب
subordinate (n)	tābiʿ (m)	تابع
colleague	zamīl (m)	زميل
acquaintance (person)	maʿruf (m)	معروف
fellow traveler	rafīq safar (m)	رفيق سفر
classmate	zamīl fiṣ ṣaff (m)	زميل في الصفّ
neighbor (masc.)	ʒār (m)	جار
neighbor (fem.)	ʒāra (f)	جارة
neighbors	ʒirān (pl)	جيران

HUMAN BODY. MEDICINE

61. Head

head	ra's (m)	رأس
face	waʒh (m)	وجه
nose	anf (m)	أنف
mouth	fam (m)	فم
eye	'ayn (f)	عين
eyes	'uyūn (pl)	عيون
pupil	ḥadaqa (f)	حدقة
eyebrow	ḥāʒib (m)	حاجب
eyelash	rimʃ (m)	رمش
eyelid	ʒafn (m)	جفن
tongue	lisān (m)	لسان
tooth	sinn (f)	سنّ
lips	ʃifāh (pl)	شفاه
cheekbones	'iẓām waʒhiyya (pl)	عظام وجهيّة
gum	liθθa (f)	لِثّة
palate	ḥanak (m)	حنك
nostrils	minχarān (du)	منخران
chin	ðaqan (m)	ذقن
jaw	fakk (m)	فكّ
cheek	χadd (m)	خدّ
forehead	ʒabha (f)	جبهة
temple	ṣudɣ (m)	صدغ
ear	uðun (f)	أذن
back of the head	qafa (m)	قفا
neck	raqaba (f)	رقبة
throat	ḥalq (m)	حلق
hair	ʃaʿr (m)	شعر
hairstyle	tasrīḥa (f)	تسريحة
haircut	tasrīḥa (f)	تسريحة
wig	barūka (f)	باروكة
mustache	ʃawārib (pl)	شوارب
beard	liḥya (f)	لحية
to have (a beard, etc.)	'indahu	عنده
braid	ḍifira (f)	ضفيرة
sideburns	sawālif (pl)	سوالف
red-haired (adj)	aḥmar aʃ ʃaʿr	أحمر الشعر

gray (hair)	abyaḍ	أبيض
bald (adj)	aṣlaʿ	أصلع
bald patch	ṣalaʿ (m)	صلع
ponytail	ðayl ḥiṣān (m)	ذيل حصان
bangs	quṣṣa (f)	قصّة

62. Human body

hand	yad (m)	يد
arm	ðirāʿ (f)	ذراع
finger	iṣbaʿ (m)	إصبع
toe	iṣbaʿ al qadam (m)	إصبع القدم
thumb	ibhām (m)	إبهام
little finger	xunṣur (m)	خنصر
nail	ẓufr (m)	ظفر
fist	qabḍa (f)	قبضة
palm	kaff (f)	كفّ
wrist	miʿṣam (m)	معصم
forearm	sāʿid (m)	ساعد
elbow	mirfaq (m)	مرفق
shoulder	katf (f)	كتف
leg	riʒl (f)	رجل
foot	qadam (f)	قدم
knee	rukba (f)	ركبة
calf (part of leg)	sammāna (f)	سمّانة
hip	faxð (f)	فخذ
heel	ʿaqb (m)	عقب
body	ʒism (m)	جسم
stomach	baṭn (m)	بطن
chest	ṣadr (m)	صدر
breast	θady (m)	ثدي
flank	ʒamb (m)	جنب
back	ẓahr (m)	ظهر
lower back	asfal aẓ ẓahr (m)	أسفل الظهر
waist	xaṣr (m)	خصر
navel (belly button)	surra (f)	سرّة
buttocks	ardāf (pl)	أرداف
bottom	dubr (m)	دبر
beauty mark	ʃāma (f)	شامة
birthmark (café au lait spot)	waḥma	وحمة
tattoo	waʃm (m)	وشم
scar	nadba (f)	ندبة

63. Diseases

sickness	maraḍ (m)	مرض
to be sick	maraḍ	مرض
health	ṣiḥḥa (f)	صحّة
runny nose (coryza)	zukām (m)	زكام
tonsillitis	iltihāb al lawzatayn (m)	التهاب اللوزتين
cold (illness)	bard (m)	برد
to catch a cold	aṣābahu al bard	أصابه البرد
bronchitis	iltihāb al qaṣabāt (m)	إلتهاب القصبات
pneumonia	iltihāb ar ri'atayn (m)	إلتهاب الرئتين
flu, influenza	inflūnza (f)	إنفلونزا
nearsighted (adj)	qaṣīr an naẓar	قصير النظر
farsighted (adj)	ba'īd an naẓar	بعيد النظر
strabismus (crossed eyes)	ḥawal (m)	حول
cross-eyed (adj)	aḥwal	أحول
cataract	katarakt (f)	كاتاراكت
glaucoma	glawkūma (f)	جلوكوما
stroke	sakta (f)	سكتة
heart attack	iḥtijā' (m)	إحتشاء
myocardial infarction	nawba qalbiya (f)	نوبة قلبية
paralysis	ʃalal (m)	شلل
to paralyze (vt)	ʃall	شلَ
allergy	ḥassāsiyya (f)	حسّاسيّة
asthma	rabw (m)	ربو
diabetes	ad dā' as sukkariy (m)	الداء السكّريّ
toothache	alam al asnān (m)	ألم الأسنان
caries	naxar al asnān (m)	نخر الأسنان
diarrhea	ishāl (m)	إسهال
constipation	imsāk (m)	إمساك
stomach upset	'usr al haḍm (m)	عسر الهضم
food poisoning	tasammum (m)	تسمّم
to get food poisoning	tasammam	تسمّم
arthritis	iltihāb al mafāṣil (m)	إلتهاب المفاصل
rickets	kusāḥ al aṭfāl (m)	كساح الأطفال
rheumatism	riumatizm (m)	روماتزم
atherosclerosis	taṣṣallub aʃ ʃarayīn (m)	تصلّب الشرايين
gastritis	iltihāb al ma'ida (m)	إلتهاب المعدة
appendicitis	iltihāb az zā'ida ad dūdiyya (m)	إلتهاب الزائدة الدوديّة
cholecystitis	iltihāb al marāra (m)	إلتهاب المرارة
ulcer	qurḥa (f)	قرحة

measles	maraḍ al ḥaṣba (m)	مرض الحصبة
rubella (German measles)	ḥaṣba almāniyya (f)	حصبة ألمانية
jaundice	yaraqān (m)	يرقان
hepatitis	iltihāb al kabd al vayrūsiy (m)	إلتهاب الكبد الفيروسيّ

schizophrenia	ʃizufrīniya (f)	شيزوفرينيا
rabies (hydrophobia)	dā' al kalb (m)	داء الكلب
neurosis	'iṣāb (m)	عصاب
concussion	irtiʒāʒ al muxx (m)	إرتجاج المخ

cancer	saraṭān (m)	سرطان
sclerosis	taṣṣallub (m)	تصلّب
multiple sclerosis	taṣṣallub muta'addid (m)	تصلّب متعدد

alcoholism	idmān al xamr (m)	إدمان الخمر
alcoholic (n)	mudmin al xamr (m)	مدمن الخمر
syphilis	sifilis az zuhariy (m)	سفلس الزهري
AIDS	al aydz (m)	الايدز

tumor	waram (m)	ورم
malignant (adj)	xabīθ	خبيث
benign (adj)	ḥamīd (m)	حميد

fever	ḥumma (f)	حمّى
malaria	malāriya (f)	ملاريا
gangrene	ɣanɣrīna (f)	غنغرينا
seasickness	duwār al baḥr (m)	دوار البحر
epilepsy	maraḍ aṣ ṣar' (m)	مرض الصرع

epidemic	wabā' (m)	وباء
typhus	tīfus (m)	تيفوس
tuberculosis	maraḍ as sull (m)	مرض السلّ
cholera	kulīra (f)	كوليرا
plague (bubonic ~)	ṭā'ūn (m)	طاعون

64. Symptoms. Treatments. Part 1

symptom	'araḍ (m)	عرض
temperature	ḥarāra (f)	حرارة
high temperature (fever)	ḥumma (f)	حمّى
pulse	nabḍ (m)	نبض

dizziness (vertigo)	dawxa (f)	دوخة
hot (adj)	ḥārr	حارّ
shivering	nafaḍān (m)	نفضان
pale (e.g., ~ face)	aṣfar	أصفر

| cough | su'āl (m) | سعال |
| to cough (vi) | sa'al | سعل |

to sneeze (vi)	ʻaṭas	عطس
faint	iɣmāʼ (m)	إغماء
to faint (vi)	ɣumiya ʻalayh	غمي عليه

bruise (hématome)	kadma (f)	كدمة
bump (lump)	tawarrum (m)	تورّم
to bang (bump)	iṣṭadam	إصطدم
contusion (bruise)	raḍḍ (m)	رضّ
to get a bruise	taraḍḍaḍ	ترضّض

to limp (vi)	ʻaraʒ	عرج
dislocation	χalʻ (m)	خلع
to dislocate (vt)	χalaʻ	خلع
fracture	kasr (m)	كسر
to have a fracture	inkasar	إنكسر

cut (e.g., paper ~)	ʒurḥ (m)	جرح
to cut oneself	ʒaraḥ nafsah	جرح نفسه
bleeding	nazf (m)	نزف

| burn (injury) | ḥarq (m) | حرق |
| to get burned | taʃayyat | تشيط |

to prick (vt)	waχaz	وخز
to prick oneself	waχaz nafsah	وخز نفسه
to injure (vt)	aṣāb	أصاب
injury	iṣāba (f)	إصابة
wound	ʒurḥ (m)	جرح
trauma	ṣadma (f)	صدمة

to be delirious	haða	هذى
to stutter (vi)	talaʻsam	تلعثم
sunstroke	ḍarbat ʃams (f)	ضربة شمس

65. Symptoms. Treatments. Part 2

| pain, ache | alam (m) | ألم |
| splinter (in foot, etc.) | ʃaẓiyya (f) | شظيّة |

sweat (perspiration)	ʻirq (m)	عرق
to sweat (perspire)	ʻariq	عرق
vomiting	taqayyuʻ (m)	تقيّؤ
convulsions	taʃannuʒāt (pl)	تشنّجات

pregnant (adj)	ḥāmil	حامل
to be born	wulid	وُلد
delivery, labor	wilāda (f)	ولادة
to deliver (~ a baby)	walad	ولد
abortion	iʒhāḍ (m)	إجهاض
breathing, respiration	tanaffus (m)	تنفّس

in-breath (inhalation)	istinʃāq (m)	إستنشاق
out-breath (exhalation)	zafīr (m)	زفير
to exhale (breathe out)	zafar	زفر
to inhale (vi)	istanʃaq	إستنشق

disabled person	mu'āq (m)	معاق
cripple	muq'ad (m)	مقعد
drug addict	mudmin muxaddirāt (m)	مدمن مخدّرات

deaf (adj)	aṭraʃ	أطرش
mute (adj)	axras	أخرس
deaf mute (adj)	aṭraʃ axras	أطرش أخرس

mad, insane (adj)	maʒnūn (m)	مجنون
madman (demented person)	maʒnūn (m)	مجنون
madwoman	maʒnūna (f)	مجنونة
to go insane	ʒunn	جنّ

gene	ʒīn (m)	جين
immunity	manā'a (f)	مناعة
hereditary (adj)	wirāθiy	وراثيّ
congenital (adj)	xilqiy munð al wilāda	خلقيّ منذ الولادة

virus	virūs (m)	فيروس
microbe	mikrūb (m)	ميكروب
bacterium	ʒurθūma (f)	جرثومة
infection	'adwa (f)	عدوى

66. Symptoms. Treatments. Part 3

| hospital | mustaʃfa (m) | مستشفى |
| patient | marīḍ (m) | مريض |

diagnosis	taʃxīṣ (m)	تشخيص
cure	'ilāʒ (m)	علاج
medical treatment	'ilāʒ (m)	علاج
to get treatment	ta'ālaʒ	تعالج
to treat (~ a patient)	'ālaʒ	عالج
to nurse (look after)	marraḍ	مرّض
care (nursing ~)	'ināya (f)	عناية

operation, surgery	'amaliyya ʒaraḥiyya (f)	عمليّة جرحيّة
to bandage (head, limb)	ḍammad	ضمّد
bandaging	taḍmīd (m)	تضميد

vaccination	talqīḥ (m)	تلقيح
to vaccinate (vt)	laqqaḥ	لقّح
injection, shot	ḥuqna (f)	حقنة
to give an injection	ḥaqan ibra	حقن إبرة

attack	nawba (f)	نوبة
amputation	batr (m)	بتر
to amputate (vt)	batar	بتر
coma	ɣaybūba (f)	غيبوبة
to be in a coma	kān fi ḥālat ɣaybūba	كان في حالة غيبوبة
intensive care	al 'ināya al murakkaza (f)	العناية المركّزة

to recover (~ from flu)	ʃufiy	شفي
condition (patient's ~)	ḥāla (f)	حالة
consciousness	wa'y (m)	وعي
memory (faculty)	ðākira (f)	ذاكرة

to pull out (tooth)	xala'	خلع
filling	haʃw (m)	حشو
to fill (a tooth)	haʃa	حشا

| hypnosis | at tanwīm al maɣnaṭīsiy (m) | التنويم المغناطيسيّ |
| to hypnotize (vt) | nawwam | نوّم |

67. Medicine. Drugs. Accessories

medicine, drug	dawā' (m)	دواء
remedy	'ilāʒ (m)	علاج
to prescribe (vt)	waṣaf	وصف
prescription	waṣfa (f)	وصفة

tablet, pill	qurṣ (m)	قرص
ointment	marham (m)	مرهم
ampule	ambūla (f)	أمبولة
mixture	dawā' ʃarāb (m)	دواء شراب
syrup	ʃarāb (m)	شراب
pill	ḥabba (f)	حبّة
powder	ðarūr (m)	ذرور

gauze bandage	ḍammāda (f)	ضمادة
cotton wool	quṭn (m)	قطن
iodine	yūd (m)	يود
Band-Aid	blāstir (m)	بلاستر
eyedropper	māṣṣat al bastara (f)	ماصّة البسترة
thermometer	tirmūmitr (m)	ترمومتر
syringe	miḥqana (f)	محقنة

| wheelchair | kursiy mutaḥarrik (m) | كرسي متحرّك |
| crutches | 'ukkāzān (du) | عكّازان |

painkiller	musakkin (m)	مسكّن
laxative	mulayyin (m)	ملين
spirits (ethanol)	iθanūl (m)	إيثانول
medicinal herbs	a'ʃāb ṭibbiyya (pl)	أعشاب طبية
herbal (~ tea)	'uʃbiy	عشبيّ

APARTMENT

68. Apartment

apartment	ʃaqqa (f)	شقَّة
room	ɣurfa (f)	غرفة
bedroom	ɣurfat an nawm (f)	غرفة النوم
dining room	ɣurfat il akl (f)	غرفة الأكل
living room	ṣālat al istiqbāl (f)	صالة الإستقبال
study (home office)	maktab (m)	مكتب
entry room	madχal (m)	مدخل
bathroom (room with a bath or shower)	ḥammām (m)	حمّام
half bath	ḥammām (m)	حمّام
ceiling	saqf (m)	سقف
floor	arḍ (f)	أرض
corner	zāwiya (f)	زاوية

69. Furniture. Interior

furniture	aθāθ (m)	أثاث
table	maktab (m)	مكتب
chair	kursiy (m)	كرسيّ
bed	sarīr (m)	سرير
couch, sofa	kanaba (f)	كنبة
armchair	kursiy (m)	كرسيّ
bookcase	χizānat kutub (f)	خزانة كتب
shelf	raff (m)	رفّ
wardrobe	dūlāb (m)	دولاب
coat rack (wall-mounted ~)	ʃammāʿa (f)	شمّاعة
coat stand	ʃammāʿa (f)	شمّاعة
bureau, dresser	dulāb adrāʒ (m)	دولاب أدراج
coffee table	ṭāwilat al qahwa (f)	طاولة القهوة
mirror	mir'āt (f)	مرآة
carpet	siʒāda (f)	سجادة
rug, small carpet	siʒāda (f)	سجادة
fireplace	midfa'a ḥā'iṭiyya (f)	مدفأة حائطيّة
candle	ʃam'a (f)	شمعة

candlestick	ʃamʿadān (m)	شمعدان
drapes	satā'ir (pl)	ستائر
wallpaper	waraq ḥī'ṭān (m)	ورق حيطان
blinds (jalousie)	haṣīrat ʃubbāk (f)	حصيرة شبّاك
table lamp	miṣbāḥ aṭ ṭāwila (m)	مصباح الطاولة
wall lamp (sconce)	miṣbāḥ al ḥā'iṭ (f)	مصباح الحائط
floor lamp	miṣbāḥ arḍiy (m)	مصباح أرضيَ
chandelier	naẓafa (f)	نجفة
leg (of chair, table)	riʒl (f)	رجل
armrest	masnad (m)	مسند
back (backrest)	masnad (m)	مسند
drawer	durʒ (m)	درج

70. Bedding

bedclothes	bayāḍāt as sarīr (pl)	بياضات السرير
pillow	wisāda (f)	وسادة
pillowcase	kīs al wisāda (m)	كيس الوسادة
duvet, comforter	baṭṭāniyya (f)	بطّانيّة
sheet	milāya (f)	ملاية
bedspread	ɣiṭā' as sarīr (m)	غطاء السرير

71. Kitchen

kitchen	maṭbax (m)	مطبخ
gas	ɣāz (m)	غاز
gas stove (range)	butuɣāz (m)	بوتوغاز
electric stove	furn kaharabā'iy (m)	فرن كهربائيَ
oven	furn (m)	فرن
microwave oven	furn al mikruwayv (m)	فرن الميكروويف
refrigerator	θallāʒa (f)	ثلاجة
freezer	frīzir (m)	فريزير
dishwasher	ɣassāla (f)	غسّالة
meat grinder	farrāmat laḥm (f)	فرّامة لحم
juicer	ʿaṣṣāra (f)	عصّارة
toaster	maḥmaṣat xubz (f)	محمصة خبز
mixer	xallāṭ (m)	خلّاط
coffee machine	mākinat ṣanʿ al qahwa (f)	ماكينة صنع القهوة
coffee pot	kanaka (f)	كنكة
coffee grinder	maṭḥanat qahwa (f)	مطحنة قهوة
kettle	barrād (m)	برّاد
teapot	barrād aʃ ʃāy (m)	برّاد الشاي

lid	ɣiṭā' (m)	غطاء
tea strainer	miṣfāt (f)	مصفاة
spoon	mil'aqa (f)	ملعقة
teaspoon	mil'aqat ʃāy (f)	ملعقة شاي
soup spoon	mil'aqa kabīra (f)	ملعقة كبيرة
fork	ʃawka (f)	شوكة
knife	sikkīn (m)	سكّين
tableware (dishes)	ṣuḥūn (pl)	صحون
plate (dinner ~)	ṭabaq (m)	طبق
saucer	ṭabaq finʒān (m)	طبق فنجان
shot glass	ka's (f)	كأس
glass (tumbler)	kubbāya (f)	كبّاية
cup	finʒān (m)	فنجان
sugar bowl	sukkariyya (f)	سكّريّة
salt shaker	mamlaḥa (f)	مملحة
pepper shaker	mabhara (f)	مبهرة
butter dish	ṣuḥn zubda (m)	صحن زبدة
stock pot (soup pot)	kassirūlla (f)	كاسرولة
frying pan (skillet)	ṭāsa (f)	طاسة
ladle	miɣrafa (f)	مغرفة
colander	miṣfāt (f)	مصفاة
tray (serving ~)	ṣīniyya (f)	صينيّة
bottle	zuʒāʒa (f)	زجاجة
jar (glass)	barṭamān (m)	برطمان
can	tanaka (f)	تنكة
bottle opener	fattāḥa (f)	فتّاحة
can opener	fattāḥa (f)	فتّاحة
corkscrew	barrīma (f)	بريّمة
filter	filtir (m)	فلتر
to filter (vt)	ṣaffa	صفّى
trash, garbage (food waste, etc.)	zubāla (f)	زبالة
trash can (kitchen ~)	ṣundūq az zubāla (m)	صندوق الزبالة

72. Bathroom

bathroom	ḥammām (m)	حمّام
water	mā' (m)	ماء
faucet	ḥanafiyya (f)	حنفيّة
hot water	mā' sāxin (m)	ماء ساخن
cold water	mā' bārid (m)	ماء بارد
toothpaste	ma'ʒūn asnān (m)	معجون أسنان

to brush one's teeth	naẓẓaf al asnān	نظّف الأسنان
toothbrush	furʃat asnān (f)	فرشة أسنان
to shave (vi)	ḥalaq	حلق
shaving foam	raɣwa lil ḥilāqa (f)	رغوة للحلاقة
razor	mūs ḥilāqa (m)	موس حلاقة
to wash (one's hands, etc.)	ɣasal	غسل
to take a bath	istaḥamm	إستحمّ
shower	dūʃ (m)	دوش
to take a shower	aҳað ad duʃ	أخذ الدش
bathtub	ḥawḍ istiḥmām (m)	حوض استحمام
toilet (toilet bowl)	mirḥāḍ (m)	مرحاض
sink (washbasin)	ḥawḍ (m)	حوض
soap	ṣābūn (m)	صابون
soap dish	ṣabbāna (f)	صبّانة
sponge	līfa (f)	ليفة
shampoo	ʃāmbū (m)	شامبو
towel	fūṭa (f)	فوطة
bathrobe	θawb ḥammām (m)	ثوب حمّام
laundry (process)	ɣasīl (m)	غسيل
washing machine	ɣassāla (f)	غسّالة
to do the laundry	ɣasal al malābis	غسل الملابس
laundry detergent	masḥūq ɣasīl (m)	مسحوق غسيل

73. Household appliances

TV set	tilivizyūn (m)	تليفزيون
tape recorder	ʒihāz tasʒīl (m)	جهاز تسجيل
VCR (video recorder)	ʒihāz tasʒīl vidiyu (m)	جهاز تسجيل فيديو
radio	ʒihāz radiyu (m)	جهاز راديو
player (CD, MP3, etc.)	blayir (m)	بلاير
video projector	ʿāriḍ vidiyu (m)	عارض فيديو
home movie theater	sinima manziliyya (f)	سينما منزليّة
DVD player	di vi di (m)	دي في دي
amplifier	mukabbir aṣ ṣawt (m)	مكبّر الصوت
video game console	ʾatāri (m)	أتاري
video camera	kamira vidiyu (f)	كاميرا فيديو
camera (photo)	kamira (f)	كاميرا
digital camera	kamira diʒital (f)	كاميرا ديجيتال
vacuum cleaner	miknasa kahrabāʾiyya (f)	مكنسة كهربائيّة
iron (e.g., steam ~)	makwāt (f)	مكواة
ironing board	lawḥat kayy (f)	لوحة كيّ

telephone	hātif (m)	هاتف
cell phone	hātif maḥmūl (m)	هاتف محمول
typewriter	'āla katiba (f)	آلة كاتبة
sewing machine	'ālat al xiyāṭa (f)	آلة الخياطة

microphone	mikrufūn (m)	ميكروفون
headphones	sammā'āt ra'siya (pl)	سمّاعات رأسيّة
remote control (TV)	rimuwt kuntrūl (m)	ريموت كنترول

CD, compact disc	si di (m)	سي دي
cassette, tape	ʃarīṭ (m)	شريط
vinyl record	usṭuwāna (f)	أسطوانة

THE EARTH. WEATHER

74. Outer space

space	faḍā' (m)	فضاء
space (as adj)	faḍā'iy	فضائيَ
outer space	faḍā' (m)	فضاء
world	'ālam (m)	عالم
universe	al kawn (m)	الكون
galaxy	al maȝarra (f)	المجرَة
star	naȝm (m)	نجم
constellation	burȝ (m)	برج
planet	kawkab (m)	كوكب
satellite	qamar ṣinā'iy (m)	قمر صناعيَ
meteorite	haȝar nayzakiy (m)	حجر نيزكيَ
comet	muðannab (m)	مذنب
asteroid	kuwaykib (m)	كويكب
orbit	madār (m)	مدار
to revolve (~ around the Earth)	dār	دار
atmosphere	al ɣilāf al ȝawwiy (m)	الغلاف الجوَيَ
the Sun	aʃ ʃams (f)	الشمس
solar system	al maȝmū'a aʃ ʃamsiyya (f)	المجموعة الشمسيَة
solar eclipse	kusūf aʃ ʃams (m)	كسوف الشمس
the Earth	al arḍ (f)	الأرض
the Moon	al qamar (m)	القمر
Mars	al mirrīχ (m)	المرَيخ
Venus	az zahra (f)	الزهرة
Jupiter	al muʃtari (m)	المشتري
Saturn	zuḥal (m)	زحل
Mercury	'aṭārid (m)	عطارد
Uranus	urānus (m)	اورانوس
Neptune	nibtūn (m)	نبتون
Pluto	blūtu (m)	بلوتو
Milky Way	darb at tabbāna (m)	درب التَبَانة
Great Bear (Ursa Major)	ad dubb al akbar (m)	الدبَ الأكبر
North Star	naȝm al 'qutb (m)	نجم القطب
Martian	sākin al mirrīχ (m)	ساكن المرَيخ

extraterrestrial (n)	faḍā'iy (m)	فضائيّ
alien	faḍā'iy (m)	فضائيّ
flying saucer	ṭabaq ṭā'ir (m)	طبق طائر
spaceship	markaba faḍā'iyya (f)	مركبة فضائيّة
space station	maḥaṭṭat faḍā' (f)	محطّة فضاء
blast-off	inṭilāq (m)	إنطلاق
engine	mutūr (m)	موتور
nozzle	manfaθ (m)	منفث
fuel	wuqūd (m)	وقود
cockpit, flight deck	kabīna (f)	كابينة
antenna	hawā'iy (m)	هوائيّ
porthole	kuwwa mustadīra (f)	كوّة مستديرة
solar panel	lawḥ ʃamsiy (m)	لوح شمسيّ
spacesuit	baðlat al faḍā' (f)	بذلة الفضاء
weightlessness	in'idām al wazn (m)	إنعدام الوزن
oxygen	uksiʒīn (m)	أكسجين
docking (in space)	rasw (m)	رسو
to dock (vi, vt)	rasa	رسا
observatory	marṣad (m)	مرصد
telescope	tiliskūp (m)	تلسكوب
to observe (vt)	rāqab	راقب
to explore (vt)	istakʃaf	إستكشف

75. The Earth

the Earth	al arḍ (f)	الأرض
the globe (the Earth)	al kura al arḍiyya (f)	الكرة الأرضيّة
planet	kawkab (m)	كوكب
atmosphere	al ɣilāf al ʒawwiy (m)	الغلاف الجوّيّ
geography	ʒuɣrāfiya (f)	جغرافيا
nature	ṭabīʿa (f)	طبيعة
globe (table ~)	namūðaʒ lil kura al arḍiyya (m)	نموذج للكرة الأرضيّة
map	xarīṭa (f)	خريطة
atlas	aṭlas (m)	أطلس
Europe	urūbba (f)	أوروبّا
Asia	'āsiya (f)	آسيا
Africa	afrīqiya (f)	أفريقيا
Australia	usturāliya (f)	أستراليا
America	amrīka (f)	أمريكا
North America	amrīka aʃ ʃimāliyya (f)	أمريكا الشماليّة

South America	amrīka al ʒanūbiyya (f)	أمريكا الجنوبيّة
Antarctica	al quṭb al ʒanūbiy (m)	القطب الجنوبيّ
the Arctic	al quṭb aʃ ʃimāliy (m)	القطب الشمالي

76. Cardinal directions

north	ʃimāl (m)	شمال
to the north	ilaʃ ʃimāl	إلى الشمال
in the north	fiʃ ʃimāl	في الشمال
northern (adj)	ʃimāliy	شماليَ

south	ʒanūb (m)	جنوب
to the south	ilal ʒanūb	إلى الجنوب
in the south	fil ʒanūb	في الجنوب
southern (adj)	ʒanūbiy	جنوبيَ

west	ɣarb (m)	غرب
to the west	ilal ɣarb	إلى الغرب
in the west	fil ɣarb	في الغرب
western (adj)	ɣarbiy	غربي

east	ʃarq (m)	شرق
to the east	ilaʃ ʃarq	إلى الشرق
in the east	fiʃ ʃarq	في الشرق
eastern (adj)	ʃarqiy	شرقيَ

77. Sea. Ocean

sea	baḥr (m)	بحر
ocean	muḥīṭ (m)	محيط
gulf (bay)	xalīʒ (m)	خليج
straits	maḍīq (m)	مضيق

land (solid ground)	barr (m)	برَ
continent (mainland)	qārra (f)	قارّة
island	ʒazīra (f)	جزيرة
peninsula	ʃibh ʒazīra (f)	شبه جزيرة
archipelago	maʒmūʿat ʒuzur (f)	مجموعة جزر

bay, cove	xalīʒ (m)	خليج
harbor	mīnā' (m)	ميناء
lagoon	buḥayra ʃāṭi'a (f)	بحيرة شاطئة
cape	ra's (m)	رأس

atoll	ʒazīra marʒāniyya istiwā'iyya (f)	جزيرة مرجانيّة إستوائيّة
reef	ʃiʿāb (pl)	شعاب
coral	murʒān (m)	مرجان

coral reef	ʃiʻāb marӡāniyya (pl)	شعاب مرجانيّة
deep (adj)	ʻamīq	عميق
depth (deep water)	ʻumq (m)	عمق
abyss	mahwāt (f)	مهواة
trench (e.g., Mariana ~)	χandaq (m)	خندق
current (Ocean ~)	tayyār (m)	تيّار
to surround (bathe)	aḥāṭ	أحاط
shore	sāḥil (m)	ساحل
coast	sāḥil (m)	ساحل
flow (flood tide)	madd (m)	مدّ
ebb (ebb tide)	ӡazr (m)	جزر
shoal	miyāh ḍaḥla (f)	مياه ضحلة
bottom (~ of the sea)	qāʻ (m)	قاع
wave	mawӡa (f)	موجة
crest (~ of a wave)	qimmat mawӡa (f)	قمّة موجة
spume (sea foam)	zabad al baḥr (m)	زبد البحر
storm (sea storm)	ʻāṣifa (f)	عاصفة
hurricane	iʻṣār (m)	إعصار
tsunami	tsunāmi (m)	تسونامي
calm (dead ~)	hudūʼ (m)	هدوء
quiet, calm (adj)	hādiʼ	هادئ
pole	quṭb (m)	قطب
polar (adj)	quṭby	قطبيّ
latitude	ʻarḍ (m)	عرض
longitude	ṭūl (m)	طول
parallel	mutawāzi (m)	متواز
equator	χaṭṭ al istiwāʼ (m)	خط الإستواء
sky	samāʼ (f)	سماء
horizon	ufuq (m)	أفق
air	hawāʼ (m)	هواء
lighthouse	manāra (f)	منارة
to dive (vi)	ɣāṣ	غاص
to sink (ab. boat)	ɣariq	غرق
treasures	kunūz (pl)	كنوز

78. Seas' and Oceans' names

Atlantic Ocean	al muḥīṭ al aṭlasiy (m)	المحيط الأطلسيّ
Indian Ocean	al muḥīṭ al hindiy (m)	المحيط الهنديّ
Pacific Ocean	al muḥīṭ al hādiʼ (m)	المحيط الهادئ
Arctic Ocean	al muḥīṭ il mutaӡammid aʃ ʃimāliy (m)	المحيط المتجمّد الشماليّ

Black Sea	al baḥr al aswad (m)	البحر الأسود
Red Sea	al baḥr al aḥmar (m)	البحر الأحمر
Yellow Sea	al baḥr al aṣfar (m)	البحر الأصفر
White Sea	al baḥr al abyaḍ (m)	البحر الأبيض
Caspian Sea	baḥr qazwīn (m)	بحر قزوين
Dead Sea	al baḥr al mayyit (m)	البحر الميّت
Mediterranean Sea	al baḥr al abyaḍ al mutawassiṭ (m)	البحر الأبيض المتوسّط
Aegean Sea	baḥr ʾīʒah (m)	بحر إيجة
Adriatic Sea	al baḥr al adriyatīkiy (m)	البحر الأدرياتيكيّ
Arabian Sea	baḥr al ʿarab (m)	بحر العرب
Sea of Japan	baḥr al yabān (m)	بحر اليابان
Bering Sea	baḥr birinʒ (m)	بحر بيرينغ
South China Sea	baḥr aṣ sīn al ʒanūbiy (m)	بحر الصين الجنوبيّ
Coral Sea	baḥr al marʒān (m)	بحر المرجان
Tasman Sea	baḥr tasmān (m)	بحر تسمان
Caribbean Sea	al baḥr al karībiy (m)	البحر الكاريبيّ
Barents Sea	baḥr barints (m)	بحر بارينس
Kara Sea	baḥr kara (m)	بحر كارا
North Sea	baḥr aʃ ʃimāl (m)	بحر الشمال
Baltic Sea	al baḥr al balṭīq (m)	البحر البلطيق
Norwegian Sea	baḥr an narwīʒ (m)	بحر النرويج

79. Mountains

mountain	ʒabal (m)	جبل
mountain range	silsilat ʒibāl (f)	سلسلة جبال
mountain ridge	qimam ʒabaliyya (pl)	قمم جبليّة
summit, top	qimma (f)	قمّة
peak	qimma (f)	قمة
foot (~ of the mountain)	asfal (m)	أسفل
slope (mountainside)	munḥadar (m)	منحدر
volcano	burkān (m)	بركان
active volcano	burkān naʃīṭ (m)	بركان نشط
dormant volcano	burkān χāmid (m)	بركان خامد
eruption	θawrān (m)	ثوران
crater	fūhat al burkān (f)	فوهة البركان
magma	māχma (f)	ماغما
lava	ḥumam burkāniyya (pl)	حمم بركانيّة
molten (~ lava)	munṣahira	منصهرة
canyon	talʿa (m)	تلعة

87

gorge	wādi ḍayyiq (m)	واد ضيّق
crevice	ʃaqq (m)	شقّ
abyss (chasm)	hāwiya (f)	هاوية

pass, col	mamarr ӡabaliy (m)	ممرّ جبليّ
plateau	haḍba (f)	هضبة
cliff	ӡurf (m)	جرف
hill	tall (m)	تلّ

glacier	nahr ӡalīdiy (m)	نهر جليديّ
waterfall	ʃallāl (m)	شلّال
geyser	fawwāra ḥarra (m)	فوّارة حارّة
lake	buḥayra (f)	بحيرة

plain	sahl (m)	سهل
landscape	manẓar ṭabīʿiy (m)	منظر طبيعيّ
echo	ṣada (m)	صدى

alpinist	mutasalliq al ӡibāl (m)	متسلّق الجبال
rock climber	mutasalliq ṣuxūr (m)	متسلّق صخور
to conquer (in climbing)	taɣallab ʿala	تغلّب على
climb (an easy ~)	tasalluq (m)	تسلّق

80. Mountains names

The Alps	ӡibāl al alb (pl)	جبال الألب
Mont Blanc	mūn blūn (m)	مون بلون
The Pyrenees	ӡibāl al barānis (pl)	جبال البرانس

The Carpathians	ӡibāl al karbāt (pl)	جبال الكاربات
The Ural Mountains	ӡibāl al ʾūrāl (pl)	جبال الأورال
The Caucasus Mountains	ӡibāl al qawqāz (pl)	جبال القوقاز
Mount Elbrus	ӡabal ilbrūs (m)	جبل إلبروس

The Altai Mountains	ӡibāl altāy (pl)	جبال ألتاي
The Tian Shan	ӡibāl tian ʃan (pl)	جبال تيان شان
The Pamir Mountains	ӡibāl bamīr (pl)	جبال بامير
The Himalayas	himalāya (pl)	هيمالايا
Mount Everest	ӡabal ivirist (m)	جبل افرست

The Andes	ӡibāl al andīz (pl)	جبال الأنديز
Mount Kilimanjaro	ӡabal kilimanӡāru (m)	جبل كليمنجارو

81. Rivers

river	nahr (m)	نهر
spring (natural source)	ʿayn (m)	عين
riverbed (river channel)	maӡra an nahr (m)	مجرى النهر

basin (river valley)	ḥawḍ (m)	حوض
to flow into …	ṣabb fi …	صبّ في...
tributary	rāfid (m)	رافد
bank (of river)	ḍiffa (f)	ضفة
current (stream)	tayyār (m)	تيّار
downstream (adv)	f ittiʒāh maʒra an nahr	في إتجاه مجرى النهر
upstream (adv)	ḍidd at tayyār	ضد التيّار
inundation	ɣamr (m)	غمر
flooding	fayaḍān (m)	فيضان
to overflow (vi)	fāḍ	فاض
to flood (vt)	ɣamar	غمر
shallow (shoal)	miyāh ḍaḥla (f)	مياه ضحلة
rapids	munḥadar an nahr (m)	منحدر النهر
dam	sadd (m)	سدّ
canal	qanāt (f)	قناة
reservoir (artificial lake)	χazzān māʼiy (m)	خزّان مائيّ
sluice, lock	hawīs (m)	هويس
water body (pond, etc.)	masṭaḥ māʼiy (m)	مسطح مائيّ
swamp (marshland)	mustanqaʻ (m)	مستنقع
bog, marsh	mustanqaʻ (m)	مستنقع
whirlpool	dawwāma (f)	دوّامة
stream (brook)	ʒadwal māʼiy (m)	جدول مائيّ
drinking (ab. water)	aʃ ʃurb	الشرب
fresh (~ water)	ʻaðb	عذب
ice	ʒalīd (m)	جليد
to freeze over (ab. river, etc.)	taʒammad	تجمّد

82. Rivers' names

Seine	nahr as sīn (m)	نهر السين
Loire	nahr al lua:r (m)	نهر اللوار
Thames	nahr at tīmz (m)	نهر التيمز
Rhine	nahr ar rayn (m)	نهر الراين
Danube	nahr ad danūb (m)	نهر الدانوب
Volga	nahr al vulɣa (m)	نهر الفولغا
Don	nahr ad dūn (m)	نهر الدون
Lena	nahr līna (m)	نهر لينا
Yellow River	an nahr al aṣfar (m)	النهر الأصفر
Yangtze	nahr al yanχtsi (m)	نهر اليانغتسي

Mekong	nahr al mikunɣ (m)	نهر الميكونغ
Ganges	nahr al ɣānʒ (m)	نهر الغانج
Nile River	nahr an nīl (m)	نهر النيل
Congo River	nahr al kunɣu (m)	نهر الكونغو
Okavango River	nahr ukavanʒu (m)	نهر اوكافانجو
Zambezi River	nahr az zambizi (m)	نهر الزمبيزي
Limpopo River	nahr limbubu (m)	نهر ليمبوبو
Mississippi River	nahr al mississibbi (m)	نهر الميسيسيبي

83. Forest

forest, wood	ɣāba (f)	غابة
forest (as adj)	ɣāba	غابة
thick forest	ɣāba kaθīfa (f)	غابة كثيفة
grove	ɣāba ṣaɣīra (f)	غابة صغيرة
forest clearing	minṭaqa uzīlat minha al afʒār (f)	منطقة أزيلت منها الأشجار
thicket	aʒama (f)	أجمة
scrubland	fuʒayrāt (pl)	شجيرات
footpath (troddenpath)	mamarr (m)	ممرّ
gully	wādi ḍayyiq (m)	واد ضيّق
tree	faʒara (f)	شجرة
leaf	waraqa (f)	ورقة
leaves (foliage)	waraq (m)	ورق
fall of leaves	tasāquṭ al awrāq (m)	تساقط الأوراق
to fall (ab. leaves)	saqaṭ	سقط
top (of the tree)	ra's (m)	رأس
branch	ɣuṣn (m)	غصن
bough	ɣuṣn (m)	غصن
bud (on shrub, tree)	bur'um (m)	برعم
needle (of pine tree)	fawka (f)	شوكة
pine cone	kūz aṣ ṣanawbar (m)	كوز الصنوبر
hollow (in a tree)	ʒawf (m)	جوف
nest	'uʃʃ (m)	عشّ
burrow (animal hole)	ʒuḥr (m)	جحر
trunk	ʒiðʿ (m)	جذع
root	ʒiðr (m)	جذر
bark	liḥā' (m)	لحاء
moss	ṭuḥlub (m)	طحلب
to uproot (remove trees or tree stumps)	iqtala'	إقتلع

to chop down	qaṭaʿ	قطع
to deforest (vt)	azāl al yābāt	أزال الغابات
tree stump	ʒiðʿ aʃ ʃaʒara (m)	جذع الشجرة
campfire	nār muxayyam (m)	نار مخيّم
forest fire	ḥarīq yāba (m)	حريق غابة
to extinguish (vt)	aṭfaʾ	أطفأ
forest ranger	ḥāris al yāba (m)	حارس الغابة
protection	ḥimāya (f)	حماية
to protect (~ nature)	ḥama	حمى
poacher	sāriq aṣ ṣayd (m)	سارق الصيد
steel trap	maṣyada (f)	مصيدة
to gather, to pick (vt)	ʒamaʿ	جمع
to lose one's way	tāh	تاه

84. Natural resources

natural resources	θarawāt ṭabīʿiyya (pl)	ثروات طبيعيّة
minerals	maʿādin (pl)	معادن
deposits	makāmin (pl)	مكامن
field (e.g., oilfield)	ḥaql (m)	حقل
to mine (extract)	istaxraʒ	إستخرج
mining (extraction)	istixrāʒ (m)	إستخراج
ore	xām (m)	خام
mine (e.g., for coal)	manʒam (m)	منجم
shaft (mine ~)	manʒam (m)	منجم
miner	ʿāmil manʒam (m)	عامل منجم
gas (natural ~)	yāz (m)	غاز
gas pipeline	xaṭṭ anābīb yāz (m)	خط أنابيب غاز
oil (petroleum)	naft (m)	نفط
oil pipeline	anābīb an naft (pl)	أنابيب النفط
oil well	biʾr an naft (m)	بئر النفط
derrick (tower)	ḥaffāra (f)	حفّارة
tanker	nāqilat an naft (f)	ناقلة النفط
sand	raml (m)	رمل
limestone	ḥaʒar kalsiy (m)	حجر كلسيّ
gravel	ḥaṣa (m)	حصى
peat	xaθθ faḥm nabātiy (m)	خثّ فحم نباتيّ
clay	ṭīn (m)	طين
coal	faḥm (m)	فحم
iron (ore)	ḥadīd (m)	حديد
gold	ðahab (m)	ذهب
silver	fiḍḍa (f)	فضّة

nickel	nikil (m)	نيكل
copper	nuḥās (m)	نحاس
zinc	zink (m)	زنك
manganese	manɣanīz (m)	منغنيز
mercury	zi'baq (m)	زئبق
lead	ruṣāṣ (m)	رصاص
mineral	ma'dan (m)	معدن
crystal	ballūra (f)	بلّورة
marble	ruxām (m)	رخام
uranium	yurānuim (m)	يورانيوم

85. Weather

weather	ṭaqs (m)	طقس
weather forecast	naʃra ʒawwiyya (f)	نشرة جوّية
temperature	ḥarāra (f)	حرارة
thermometer	tirmūmitr (m)	ترمومتر
barometer	barūmitr (m)	بارومتر
humid (adj)	raṭib	رطب
humidity	ruṭūba (f)	رطوبة
heat (extreme ~)	ḥarāra (f)	حرارة
hot (torrid)	ḥārr	حارّ
it's hot	al ʒaww ḥārr	الجوّ حارّ
it's warm	al ʒaww dāfi'	الجوّ دافئ
warm (moderately hot)	dāfi'	دافئ
it's cold	al ʒaww bārid	الجوّ بارد
cold (adj)	bārid	بارد
sun	ʃams (f)	شمس
to shine (vi)	aḍā'	أضاء
sunny (day)	muʃmis	مشمس
to come up (vi)	ʃaraq	شرق
to set (vi)	ɣarab	غرب
cloud	saḥāba (f)	سحابة
cloudy (adj)	ɣā'im	غائم
rain cloud	saḥābat maṭar (f)	سحابة مطر
somber (gloomy)	ɣā'im	غائم
rain	maṭar (m)	مطر
it's raining	innaha tamṭur	إنّها تمطر
rainy (~ day, weather)	mumṭir	ممطر
to drizzle (vi)	raðð	رذ
pouring rain	maṭar munhamir (f)	مطر منهمر
downpour	maṭar ɣazīr (m)	مطر غزير

heavy (e.g., ~ rain)	ʃadīd	شديد
puddle	birka (f)	بركة
to get wet (in rain)	ibtall	إبتلَّ
fog (mist)	ḍabāb (m)	ضباب
foggy	muḍabbab	مضبَّب
snow	θalʒ (m)	ثلج
it's snowing	innaha taθluʒ	إنَّها تثلج

86. Severe weather. Natural disasters

thunderstorm	'āṣifa ra'diyya (f)	عاصفة رعديَّة
lightning (~ strike)	barq (m)	برق
to flash (vi)	baraq	برق
thunder	ra'd (m)	رعد
to thunder (vi)	ra'ad	رعد
it's thundering	tar'ad as samā'	ترعد السماء
hail	maṭar bard (m)	مطر برد
it's hailing	tamṭur as samā' bardan	تمطر السماء بردًا
to flood (vt)	ɣamar	غمر
flood, inundation	fayaḍān (m)	فيضان
earthquake	zilzāl (m)	زلزال
tremor, quake	hazza arḍiyya (f)	هزَّة أرضيَّة
epicenter	markaz az zilzāl (m)	مركز الزلزال
eruption	θawrān (m)	ثوران
lava	ḥumam burkāniyya (pl)	حمم بركانيَّة
twister, tornado	i'ṣār (m)	إعصار
typhoon	ṭūfān (m)	طوفان
hurricane	i'ṣār (m)	إعصار
storm	'āṣifa (f)	عاصفة
tsunami	tsunāmi (m)	تسونامي
cyclone	i'ṣār (m)	إعصار
bad weather	ṭaqs sayyi' (m)	طقس سيِّء
fire (accident)	ḥarīq (m)	حريق
disaster	kāriθa (f)	كارثة
meteorite	ḥaʒar nayzakiy (m)	حجر نيزكيّ
avalanche	inhiyār θalʒiy (m)	إنهيار ثلجيّ
snowslide	inhiyār θalʒiy (m)	إنهيار ثلجيّ
blizzard	'āṣifa θalʒiyya (f)	عاصفة ثلجيَّة
snowstorm	'āṣifa θalʒiyya (f)	عاصفة ثلجيَّة

FAUNA

87. Mammals. Predators

predator	ḥayawān muftaris (m)	حيوان مفترس
tiger	namir (m)	نمر
lion	asad (m)	أسد
wolf	ði'b (m)	ذئب
fox	θaʻlab (m)	ثعلب
jaguar	namir amrīkiyَ (m)	نمر أمريكيَّ
leopard	fahd (m)	فهد
cheetah	namir ṣayyād (m)	نمر صيّاد
black panther	namir aswad (m)	نمر أسود
puma	būma (m)	بوما
snow leopard	namir aθ θulūʒ (m)	نمر الثلوج
lynx	waʃaq (m)	وشق
coyote	qayūṭ (m)	قيوط
jackal	ibn 'āwa (m)	ابن آوى
hyena	ḍabuʻ (m)	ضبع

88. Wild animals

animal	ḥayawān (m)	حيوان
beast (animal)	ḥayawān (m)	حيوان
squirrel	sinʒāb (m)	سنجاب
hedgehog	qumfuð (m)	قنفذ
hare	arnab barriy (m)	أرنب برّيَ
rabbit	arnab (m)	أرنب
badger	ɣarīr (m)	غرير
raccoon	rākūn (m)	راكون
hamster	qidād (m)	قداد
marmot	marmuṭ (m)	مرموط
mole	χuld (m)	خلد
mouse	fa'r (m)	فأر
rat	ʒurað (m)	جرذ
bat	χuffāʃ (m)	خفّاش
ermine	qāqum (m)	قاقم
sable	sammūr (m)	سمّور

marten	dalaq (m)	دلق
weasel	ibn ʿirs (m)	إبن عرس
mink	mink (m)	منك
beaver	qundus (m)	قندس
otter	quḍāʿa (f)	قضاعة
horse	ḥiṣān (m)	حصان
moose	mūz (m)	موظ
deer	ayyil (m)	أيّل
camel	ʒamal (m)	جمل
bison	bisūn (m)	بيسون
aurochs	θawr barriy (m)	ثور برّيّ
buffalo	ʒāmūs (m)	جاموس
zebra	ḥimār zarad (m)	حمار زرد
antelope	ẓabiy (m)	ظبي
roe deer	yaḥmūr (m)	يحمور
fallow deer	ayyil asmar urubbiy (m)	أيّل أسمر أوروبّيّ
chamois	ʃamwāh (f)	شاموّاه
wild boar	xinzīr barriy (m)	خنزير برّيّ
whale	ḥūt (m)	حوت
seal	fuqma (f)	فقمة
walrus	faẓẓ (m)	فظّ
fur seal	fuqmat al firāʾ (f)	فقمة الفراء
dolphin	dilfīn (m)	دلفين
bear	dubb (m)	دبّ
polar bear	dubb quṭbiy (m)	دبّ قطبيّ
panda	bānda (m)	باندا
monkey	qird (m)	قرد
chimpanzee	ʃimbanzi (m)	شيمبانزي
orangutan	urangutān (m)	أورنغوتان
gorilla	ɣurīlla (f)	غوريلا
macaque	qird al makāk (m)	قرد المكاك
gibbon	ʒibbūn (m)	جيبون
elephant	fīl (m)	فيل
rhinoceros	xartīt (m)	خرتيت
giraffe	zarāfa (f)	زرافة
hippopotamus	faras an nahr (m)	فرس النهر
kangaroo	kanɣar (m)	كنغر
koala (bear)	kuala (m)	كوالا
mongoose	nims (m)	نمس
chinchilla	ʃinʃīla (f)	شنشيلة
skunk	ẓaribān (m)	ظربان
porcupine	nīṣ (m)	نيص

89. Domestic animals

cat	qiṭṭa (f)	قطة
tomcat	ðakar al qiṭṭ (m)	ذكر القطّ
dog	kalb (m)	كلب
horse	ḥiṣān (m)	حصان
stallion (male horse)	faḥl al χayl (m)	فحل الخيل
mare	unθa al faras (f)	أنثى الفرس
cow	baqara (f)	بقرة
bull	θawr (m)	ثور
ox	θawr (m)	ثور
sheep (ewe)	χarūf (f)	خروف
ram	kabʃ (m)	كبش
goat	māʿiz (m)	ماعز
billy goat, he-goat	ðakar al māʿið (m)	ذكر الماعز
donkey	ḥimār (m)	حمار
mule	bayl (m)	بغل
pig, hog	χinzīr (m)	خنزير
piglet	χannūṣ (m)	خنّوص
rabbit	arnab (m)	أرنب
hen (chicken)	daʒāʒa (f)	دجاجة
rooster	dīk (m)	ديك
duck	baṭṭa (f)	بطة
drake	ðakar al baṭṭ (m)	ذكر البطّ
goose	iwazza (f)	إوزة
tom turkey, gobbler	dīk rūmiy (m)	ديك رومي
turkey (hen)	daʒāʒ rūmiy (m)	دجاج رومي
domestic animals	ḥayawānāt dawāʒin (pl)	حيوانات دواجن
tame (e.g., ~ hamster)	alīf	أليف
to tame (vt)	allaf	ألف
to breed (vt)	rabba	ربى
farm	mazraʿa (f)	مزرعة
poultry	ṭuyūr dāʒina (pl)	طيور داجنة
cattle	māʃiya (f)	ماشية
herd (cattle)	qaṭīʿ (m)	قطيع
stable	isṭabl χayl (m)	إسطبل خيل
pigpen	ḥaẓīrat al χanāzīr (f)	حظيرة الخنازير
cowshed	zirībat al baqar (f)	زريبة البقر
rabbit hutch	qunn al arānib (m)	قنّ الأرانب
hen house	qunn ad daʒāʒ (m)	قن الدجاج

90. Birds

bird	ṭā'ir (m)	طائر
pigeon	ḥamāma (f)	حمامة
sparrow	'uṣfūr (m)	عصفور
tit (great tit)	qurquf (m)	قرقف
magpie	'aq'aq (m)	عقعق
raven	ɣurāb aswad (m)	غراب أسود
crow	ɣurāb (m)	غراب
jackdaw	zāɣ (m)	زاغ
rook	ɣurāb al qayẓ (m)	غراب القيظ
duck	baṭṭa (f)	بطّة
goose	iwazza (f)	إوزّة
pheasant	tadarruʒ (m)	تدرج
eagle	nasr (m)	نسر
hawk	bāz (m)	باز
falcon	ṣaqr (m)	صقر
vulture	raχam (m)	رخم
condor (Andean ~)	kundūr (m)	كندور
swan	timma (m)	تمّة
crane	kurkiy (m)	كركي
stork	laqlaq (m)	لقلق
parrot	babaɣā' (m)	ببغاء
hummingbird	ṭannān (m)	طنّان
peacock	ṭāwūs (m)	طاووس
ostrich	na'āma (f)	نعامة
heron	balaʃūn (m)	بلشون
flamingo	nuḥām wardiy (m)	نحام وردي
pelican	baʒa'a (f)	بجعة
nightingale	bulbul (m)	بلبل
swallow	sunūnū (m)	سنونو
thrush	sumna (m)	سمنة
song thrush	summuna muɣarrida (m)	سمنة مغرّدة
blackbird	ʃaḥrūr aswad (m)	شحرور أسود
swift	samāma (m)	سمامة
lark	qubbara (f)	قبّرة
quail	sammān (m)	سمّان
woodpecker	naqqār al χaʃab (m)	نقّار الخشب
cuckoo	waqwāq (m)	وقواق
owl	būma (f)	بومة
eagle owl	būm urāsiy (m)	بوم أوراسيّ

wood grouse	dīk il χalanʒ (m)	ديك الخلنج
black grouse	ṭayhūʒ aswad (m)	طيهوج أسود
partridge	ḥaʒal (m)	حجل

starling	zurzūr (m)	زرزور
canary	kanāriy (m)	كناري
hazel grouse	ṭayhūʒ il bunduq (m)	طيهوج البندق
chaffinch	ʃurʃūr (m)	شرشور
bullfinch	diχnāʃ (m)	دغناش

seagull	nawras (m)	نورس
albatross	al qaṭras (m)	القطرس
penguin	biṭrīq (m)	بطريق

91. Fish. Marine animals

bream	abramīs (m)	أبراميس
carp	ʃabbūṭ (m)	شبّوط
perch	farχ (m)	فرخ
catfish	qarmūṭ (m)	قرموط
pike	samak al karāki (m)	سمك الكراكي

| salmon | salmūn (m) | سلمون |
| sturgeon | ḥafʃ (m) | حفش |

herring	rinʒa (f)	رنجة
Atlantic salmon	salmūn aṭlasiy (m)	سلمون أطلسي
mackerel	usqumriy (m)	أسقمري
flatfish	samak mufalṭaḥ (f)	سمك مفلطح

zander, pike perch	samak sandar (m)	سمك سندر
cod	qudd (m)	قدّ
tuna	tūna (f)	تونة
trout	salmūn muraqqaṭ (m)	سلمون مرقّط

eel	ḥankalīs (m)	حنكليس
electric ray	ra"ād (m)	رعّاد
moray eel	murāy (m)	موراي
piranha	birāna (f)	بيرانا

shark	qirʃ (m)	قرش
dolphin	dilfīn (m)	دلفين
whale	ḥūt (m)	حوت

crab	salṭaʿūn (m)	سلطعون
jellyfish	qindīl al baḥr (m)	قنديل البحر
octopus	uχṭubūṭ (m)	أخطبوط

| starfish | naʒmat al baḥr (f) | نجمة البحر |
| sea urchin | qumfuð al baḥr (m) | قنفذ البحر |

seahorse	ḥiṣān al baḥr (m)	فرس البحر
oyster	maḥār (m)	محار
shrimp	ʒambari (m)	جمبري
lobster	istakūza (f)	إستكوزا
spiny lobster	karkand ʃāik (m)	كركند شائك

92. Amphibians. Reptiles

snake	θuʿbān (m)	ثعبان
venomous (snake)	sāmm	سام
viper	afʿa (f)	أفعى
cobra	kūbra (m)	كوبرا
python	biθūn (m)	بيثون
boa	buwā' (f)	بواء
grass snake	θuʿbān al ʿuʃb (m)	ثعبان العشب
rattle snake	afʿa al ʒalʒala (f)	أفعى الجلجلة
anaconda	anakūnda (f)	أناكوندا
lizard	siḥliyya (f)	سحلية
iguana	iɣwāna (f)	إغوانة
monitor lizard	waral (m)	ورل
salamander	samandar (m)	سمندر
chameleon	ḥirbā' (f)	حرباء
scorpion	ʿaqrab (m)	عقرب
turtle	sulaḥfāt (f)	سلحفاة
frog	ḍifḍaʿ (m)	ضفدع
toad	ḍifḍaʿ aṭ ṭīn (m)	ضفدع الطين
crocodile	timsāḥ (m)	تمساح

93. Insects

insect, bug	ḥaʃara (f)	حشرة
butterfly	farāʃa (f)	فراشة
ant	namla (f)	نملة
fly	ðubāba (f)	ذبابة
mosquito	namūsa (f)	ناموسة
beetle	xunfusa (f)	خنفسة
wasp	dabbūr (m)	دبّور
bee	naḥla (f)	نحلة
bumblebee	naḥla ṭannāna (f)	نحلة طنّانة
gadfly (botfly)	naʿra (f)	نعرة
spider	ʿankabūt (m)	عنكبوت
spiderweb	nasīʒ ʿankabūt (m)	نسيج عنكبوت

dragonfly	yaʻsūb (m)	يعسوب
grasshopper	ʒarād (m)	جراد
moth (night butterfly)	ʻitta (f)	عتّة
cockroach	ṣurṣūr (m)	صرصور
tick	qurāda (f)	قرادة
flea	burɣūθ (m)	برغوث
midge	baʻūḍa (f)	بعوضة
locust	ʒarād (m)	جراد
snail	ḥalzūn (m)	حلزون
cricket	ṣarrār al layl (m)	صرّار الليل
lightning bug	yarāʻa muḍīʻa (f)	يراعة مضيئة
ladybug	daʻsūqa (f)	دعسوقة
cockchafer	ҳunfusa kabīra (f)	خنفسة كبيرة
leech	ʻalaqa (f)	علقة
caterpillar	yasrūʻ (m)	يسروع
earthworm	dūda (f)	دودة
larva	yaraqa (f)	يرقة

FLORA

94. Trees

tree	ʃaӡara (f)	شجرة
deciduous (adj)	nafḍiyya	نفضيّة
coniferous (adj)	ṣanawbariyya	صنوبريّة
evergreen (adj)	dā'imat al χuḍra	دائمة الخضرة
apple tree	ʃaӡarat tuffāḥ (f)	شجرة تفّاح
pear tree	ʃaӡarat kummaθra (f)	شجرة كمّثرى
cherry tree	ʃaӡarat karaz (f)	شجرة كرز
plum tree	ʃaӡarat barqūq (f)	شجرة برقوق
birch	batūla (f)	بتولا
oak	ballūṭ (f)	بلّوط
linden tree	ʃaӡarat zayzafūn (f)	شجرة زيزفون
aspen	ḥawr raӡrāӡ (m)	حور رجراج
maple	qayqab (f)	قيقب
spruce	ratinaӡ (f)	راتينج
pine	ṣanawbar (f)	صنوبر
larch	arziyya (f)	أرزيّة
fir tree	tannūb (f)	تنّوب
cedar	arz (f)	أرز
poplar	ḥawr (f)	حور
rowan	ɣubayrā' (f)	غبيراء
willow	ṣafṣāf (f)	صفصاف
alder	ӡār il mā' (m)	جار الماء
beech	zān (m)	زان
elm	dardār (f)	دردار
ash (tree)	marān (f)	مران
chestnut	kastanā' (f)	كستناء
magnolia	maɣnūliya (f)	مغنوليا
palm tree	naχla (f)	نخلة
cypress	sarw (f)	سرو
mangrove	ayka sāḥiliyya (f)	أيكة ساحليّة
baobab	bāubāb (f)	باوباب
eucalyptus	ukaliptus (f)	أوكاليبتوس
sequoia	siqūya (f)	سيكويا

95. Shrubs

bush	ʃuʒayra (f)	شجيرة
shrub	ʃuʒayrāt (pl)	شجيرات
grapevine	karma (f)	كرمة
vineyard	karam (m)	كرم
raspberry bush	tūt al ʿullayq al aḥmar (m)	توت العلّيق الأحمر
redcurrant bush	kiʃmiʃ aḥmar (m)	كشمش أحمر
gooseberry bush	ʿinab aθ θaʿlab (m)	عنب الثعلب
acacia	sanṭ (f)	سنط
barberry	amīr barīs (m)	أمير باريس
jasmine	yāsmīn (m)	ياسمين
juniper	ʿarʿar (m)	عرعر
rosebush	ʃuʒayrat ward (f)	شجيرة ورد
dog rose	ward ʒabaliy (m)	ورد جبليّ

96. Fruits. Berries

fruit	θamra (f)	ثمرة
fruits	θamr (m)	ثمر
apple	tuffāḥa (f)	تفّاحة
pear	kummaθra (f)	كمّثرى
plum	barqūq (m)	برقوق
strawberry (garden ~)	farawla (f)	فراولة
cherry	karaz (m)	كرز
grape	ʿinab (m)	عنب
raspberry	tūt al ʿullayq al aḥmar (m)	توت العلّيق الأحمر
blackcurrant	ʿinab aθ θaʿlab al aswad (m)	عنب الثعلب الأسود
redcurrant	kiʃmiʃ aḥmar (m)	كشمش أحمر
gooseberry	ʿinab aθ θaʿlab (m)	عنب الثعلب
cranberry	tūt aḥmar barriy (m)	توت أحمر برّيّ
orange	burtuqāl (m)	برتقال
mandarin	yūsufiy (m)	يوسفي
pineapple	ananās (m)	أناناس
banana	mawz (m)	موز
date	tamr (m)	تمر
lemon	laymūn (m)	ليمون
apricot	miʃmiʃ (f)	مشمش
peach	durrāq (m)	دراق
kiwi	kiwi (m)	كيوي

grapefruit	zinbāʿ (m)	زنباع
berry	ḥabba (f)	حبّة
berries	ḥabbāt (pl)	حبّات
cowberry	ʿinab aθ θawr (m)	عنب الثور
wild strawberry	farāwla barriyya (f)	فراولة برّية
bilberry	ʿinab al aḥrāʒ (m)	عنب الأحراج

97. Flowers. Plants

| flower | zahra (f) | زهرة |
| bouquet (of flowers) | bāqat zuhūr (f) | باقة زهور |

rose (flower)	warda (f)	وردة
tulip	tulīb (f)	توليب
carnation	qurumful (m)	قرنفل
gladiolus	dalbūθ (f)	دلبوث

cornflower	turunʃāh (m)	ترنشاه
harebell	ʒarīs (m)	جريس
dandelion	hindibāʾ (f)	هندباء
camomile	babunʒ (m)	بابونج

aloe	aluwwa (m)	ألوّة
cactus	ṣabbār (m)	صبّار
rubber plant, ficus	tīn (m)	تين

lily	sawsan (m)	سوسن
geranium	ibrat ar rāʿi (f)	إبرة الراعي
hyacinth	zanbaq (f)	زنبق

mimosa	mimūza (f)	ميموزا
narcissus	narʒis (f)	نرجس
nasturtium	abu xanʒar (f)	أبو خنجر

orchid	saḥlab (f)	سحلب
peony	fawniya (f)	فاوانيا
violet	banafsaʒ (f)	بنفسج

pansy	banafsaʒ muθallaθ (m)	بنفسج مثلّث
forget-me-not	ʾāðān al faʾr (pl)	آذان الفأر
daisy	uqḥuwān (f)	أقحوان

poppy	xaʃxāʃ (f)	خشخاش
hemp	qinnab (m)	قنب
mint	naʿnāʿ (m)	نعناع

lily of the valley	sawsan al wādi (m)	سوسن الوادي
snowdrop	zahrat al laban (f)	زهرة اللبن
nettle	qarrāṣ (m)	قرّاص
sorrel	ḥammāḍ (m)	حمّاض

water lily	nilūfar (m)	نيلوفر
fern	saraxs (m)	سرخس
lichen	uʃna (f)	أشنة

greenhouse (tropical ~)	dafi'a (f)	دفيئة
lawn	'uʃb (m)	عشب
flowerbed	ʒunaynat zuhūr (f)	جنينة زهور

plant	nabāt (m)	نبات
grass	'uʃb (m)	عشب
blade of grass	'uʃba (f)	عشبة

leaf	waraqa (f)	ورقة
petal	waraqat az zahra (f)	ورقة الزهرة
stem	sāq (f)	ساق
tuber	darnat nabāt (f)	درنة نبات

| young plant (shoot) | nabta saɣīra (f) | نبتة صغيرة |
| thorn | ʃawka (f) | شوكة |

to blossom (vi)	nawwar	نوّر
to fade, to wither	ðabal	ذبل
smell (odor)	rā'iḥa (f)	رائحة
to cut (flowers)	qaṭa'	قطع
to pick (a flower)	qaṭaf	قطف

98. Cereals, grains

grain	ḥubūb (pl)	حبوب
cereal crops	maḥāṣil al ḥubūb (pl)	محاصيل الحبوب
ear (of barley, etc.)	sumbula (f)	سنبلة

wheat	qamḥ (m)	قمح
rye	ʒāwdār (m)	جاودار
oats	ʃūfān (m)	شوفان
millet	duxn (m)	دخن
barley	ʃa'īr (m)	شعير

corn	ðura (f)	ذرّة
rice	urz (m)	أرز
buckwheat	ḥinṭa sawdā' (f)	حنطة سوداء

pea plant	bisilla (f)	بسلّة
kidney bean	faṣūliya (f)	فاصوليا
soy	fūl aṣ ṣūya (m)	فول الصويا
lentil	'adas (m)	عدس
beans (pulse crops)	fūl (m)	فول

COUNTRIES OF THE WORLD

99. Countries. Part 1

Afghanistan	afɣanistān (f)	أفغانستان
Albania	albāniya (f)	ألبانيا
Argentina	arʒantīn (f)	الأرجنتين
Armenia	armīniya (f)	أرمينيا
Australia	usturāliya (f)	أستراليا
Austria	an nimsa (f)	النمسا
Azerbaijan	aðarbiʒān (m)	أذربيجان
The Bahamas	ʒuzur bahāmas (pl)	جزر باهاماس
Bangladesh	banʒladīʃ (f)	بنجلاديش
Belarus	bilarūs (f)	بيلاروس
Belgium	balʒīka (f)	بلجيكا
Bolivia	bulīviya (f)	بوليفيا
Bosnia and Herzegovina	al busna wal hirsuk (f)	البوسنة والهرسك
Brazil	al brazīl (f)	البرازيل
Bulgaria	bulɣāriya (f)	بلغاريا
Cambodia	kambūdya (f)	كمبوديا
Canada	kanada (f)	كندا
Chile	tʃīli (f)	تشيلي
China	aṣ ṣīn (f)	الصين
Colombia	kulumbiya (f)	كولومبيا
Croatia	kruātiya (f)	كرواتيا
Cuba	kūba (f)	كوبا
Cyprus	qubruṣ (f)	قبرص
Czech Republic	atʃ tʃīk (f)	التشيك
Denmark	ad danimārk (f)	الدانمارك
Dominican Republic	ʒumhūriyyat ad duminikan (f)	جمهوريّة الدومينيكان
Ecuador	al iqwadūr (f)	الإكوادور
Egypt	miṣr (f)	مصر
England	inʒiltirra (f)	إنجلترّا
Estonia	istūniya (f)	إستونيا
Finland	finlanda (f)	فنلندا
France	faransa (f)	فرنسا
French Polynesia	bulinīziya al faransiyya (f)	بولينيزيا الفرنسيّة
Georgia	ʒūrʒiya (f)	جورجيا
Germany	almāniya (f)	ألمانيا
Ghana	ɣāna (f)	غانا
Great Britain	briṭāniya al ʿuẓma (f)	بريطانيا العظمى

Greece	al yūnān (f)	اليونان
Haiti	haĩti (f)	هايتي
Hungary	al maʒar (f)	المجر

100. Countries. Part 2

Iceland	'āyslanda (f)	آيسلندا
India	al hind (f)	الهند
Indonesia	indunīsiya (f)	إندونيسيا
Iran	ĩrān (f)	إيران
Iraq	al ʿirāq (m)	العراق
Ireland	irlanda (f)	أيرلندا
Israel	isrāĩl (f)	إسرائيل
Italy	iṭāliya (f)	إيطاليا

Jamaica	ʒamāyka (f)	جامايكا
Japan	al yabān (f)	اليابان
Jordan	al urdun (m)	الأردن
Kazakhstan	kazaχstān (f)	كازاخستان
Kenya	kiniya (f)	كينيا
Kirghizia	qirɣizistān (f)	قيرغيزستان
Kuwait	al kuwayt (f)	الكويت

Laos	lawus (f)	لاوس
Latvia	lātviya (f)	لاتفيا
Lebanon	lubnān (f)	لبنان
Libya	ĩbiya (f)	ليبيا
Liechtenstein	liʃtinʃtāyn (m)	ليشتنشتاين
Lithuania	litwāniya (f)	ليتوانيا
Luxembourg	luksimburɣ (f)	لوكسمبورغ

Macedonia (Republic of ~)	maqdūniya (f)	مقدونيا
Madagascar	madaɣaʃqar (f)	مدغشقر
Malaysia	malīziya (f)	ماليزيا
Malta	malṭa (f)	مالطا
Mexico	al maksīk (f)	المكسيك
Moldova, Moldavia	muldāviya (f)	مولدافيا

Monaco	munāku (f)	موناكو
Mongolia	manɣūliya (f)	منغوليا
Montenegro	al ʒabal al aswad (m)	الجبل الأسود
Morocco	al maɣrib (m)	المغرب
Myanmar	myanmār (f)	ميانمار

Namibia	namībiya (f)	ناميبيا
Nepal	nibāl (f)	نيبال
Netherlands	hulanda (f)	هولندا
New Zealand	nyu zilanda (f)	نيوزيلندا
North Korea	kūria aʃ ʃimāliyya (f)	كوريا الشماليّة
Norway	an nirwīʒ (f)	النرويج

101. Countries. Part 3

Pakistan	bakistān (f)	باكستان
Palestine	filisṭīn (f)	فلسطين
Panama	banama (f)	بنما
Paraguay	baraɣwāy (f)	باراغواي
Peru	biru (f)	بيرو
Poland	bulanda (f)	بولندا
Portugal	al burtuɣāl (f)	البرتغال
Romania	rumāniya (f)	رومانيا
Russia	rūsiya (f)	روسيا

Saudi Arabia	as saʿūdiyya (f)	السعوديّة
Scotland	iskutlanda (f)	اسكتلندا
Senegal	as siniɣāl (f)	السنغال
Serbia	ṣirbiya (f)	صربيا
Slovakia	sluvākiya (f)	سلوفاكيا
Slovenia	sluvīniya (f)	سلوفينيا

South Africa	ʒumhūriyyat afrīqiya al ʒanūbiyya (f)	جمهريّة أفريقيا الجنوبيّة
South Korea	kuriya al ʒanūbiyya (f)	كوريا الجنوبيّة
Spain	isbāniya (f)	إسبانيا
Suriname	surinām (f)	سورينام
Sweden	as suwayd (f)	السويد
Switzerland	swīsra (f)	سويسرا
Syria	sūriya (f)	سوريا

Taiwan	taywān (f)	تايوان
Tajikistan	ṭaʒīkistān (f)	طاجيكستان
Tanzania	tanzāniya (f)	تنزانيا
Tasmania	tasmāniya (f)	تاسمانيا
Thailand	taylānd (f)	تايلاند
Tunisia	tūnis (f)	تونس
Turkey	turkiya (f)	تركيا
Turkmenistan	turkmānistān (f)	تركمانستان

Ukraine	ukrāniya (f)	أوكرانيا
United Arab Emirates	al imārāt al ʿarabiyya al muttaḥida (pl)	الإمارات العربيّة المتّحدة
United States of America	al wilāyāt al muttaḥida al amrīkiyya (pl)	الولايات المتّحدة الأمريكيّة
Uruguay	uruɣwāy (f)	الأوروغواي
Uzbekistan	uzbikistān (f)	أوزيكستان

Vatican	al vatikān (m)	الفاتيكان
Venezuela	vinizwiyla (f)	فنزويلا
Vietnam	vitnām (f)	فيتنام
Zanzibar	zanʒibār (f)	زنجبار